D1084052

PRAISE FOR MORE THAN MONEY

"Nothing communicates better than a testimony unless it is a testimony which comes from the heart and goes to the heart. Jonathan opens himself up and in so doing challenges every one of us to a faith walk which is driven by his desire to be a steward of God's resources entrusted to each of us. He asks hard questions. It is a privilege to endorse this book. Be prepared to have your faith challenged (which is a very good thing). Thanks Jonathan for sharing your challenges and learned wisdom. Every reader will benefit."

RON BLUE, author, founder of Kingdom Advisors,
and Ron Blue Institute

"Stewardship: Fan or Player? In the game or watching the game? All-in or not-in? Coachable or contrite hearts?
Jonathan's use of scripture and stories powerfully remind us that Spirit-enabled, love-inspired faith in Jesus has nothing to do with money and yet everything to do with how and why we spend it.
I read the introduction and got down on my knees.
Thank you for writing this book J."

RYAN WALTER, NHL player and coach (retired)
and Leadership Coach

"I appreciate Jonathan's straightforward, blunt, and challenging approach in *More Than Money*. You might find yourself having to take a deep breath every so often and you might even have to put it down to think through what is being said before you proceed. However, I can assure you that Jonathan and Sarah are committed to live out biblical stewardship in all areas of their lives with their time, resources and God-given gifts and talents. Jonathan's passion for God's Kingdom and His people is clearly revealed in this very practical book. Prepare to be inspired to do greater things!"

GREG MUSSELMAN, Chair of the Board for VOM
(Voice of the Martyr Canada) and host on
100 Huntley Street TV Series

"There is so much good to say about what Jonathan has written. Jonathan gets right to the point, identifying what should be our response to God's love (Romans 12:1). His life stories help the reader understand and appreciate the author in a personal way, adding interest and emotion, making the read powerful and compelling. His use of scripture, Bible stories and quotes adds interest and depth to the message. I like the way Jonathan has broadened stewardship to include all the areas we steward in life, not just our finances."

GARNET WHEATON, Chair of the Board for Shareworld Global and CEO/Founder of Wheatons Canada

"This is a unique resource that hopefully will prove helpful and encouraging to others on their stewardship journey. We don't need another typical book on stewardship, that is why I like what Jonathan has done! Sharing his own journey and stories in the midst of the content, gives this book a feeling of authenticity, and communicates that the stewardship journey is a personal journey that must be worked through."

TONY STINSON, CEO of Kingdom Advisors Worldwide

"Jonathan shares openly and insightfully about his journey into Christian stewardship. I never realized there were so many dimensions to this important journey. This book is both a blessing and a challenge to all of us."

GLEN SMELTZER, CEO Teen Challenge Canada Inc.

"Stewardship - when you hear the word you may think it's just another book about managing money. Jonathan reveals in this book that a deeper understanding of stewardship is the key to living a fulfilled life. His zeal for stewarding life is convicting, yet refreshing and insightful."

LORNE ROBINSON, National Director-Canada of Kingdom Advisors

MORE THAN MONEY

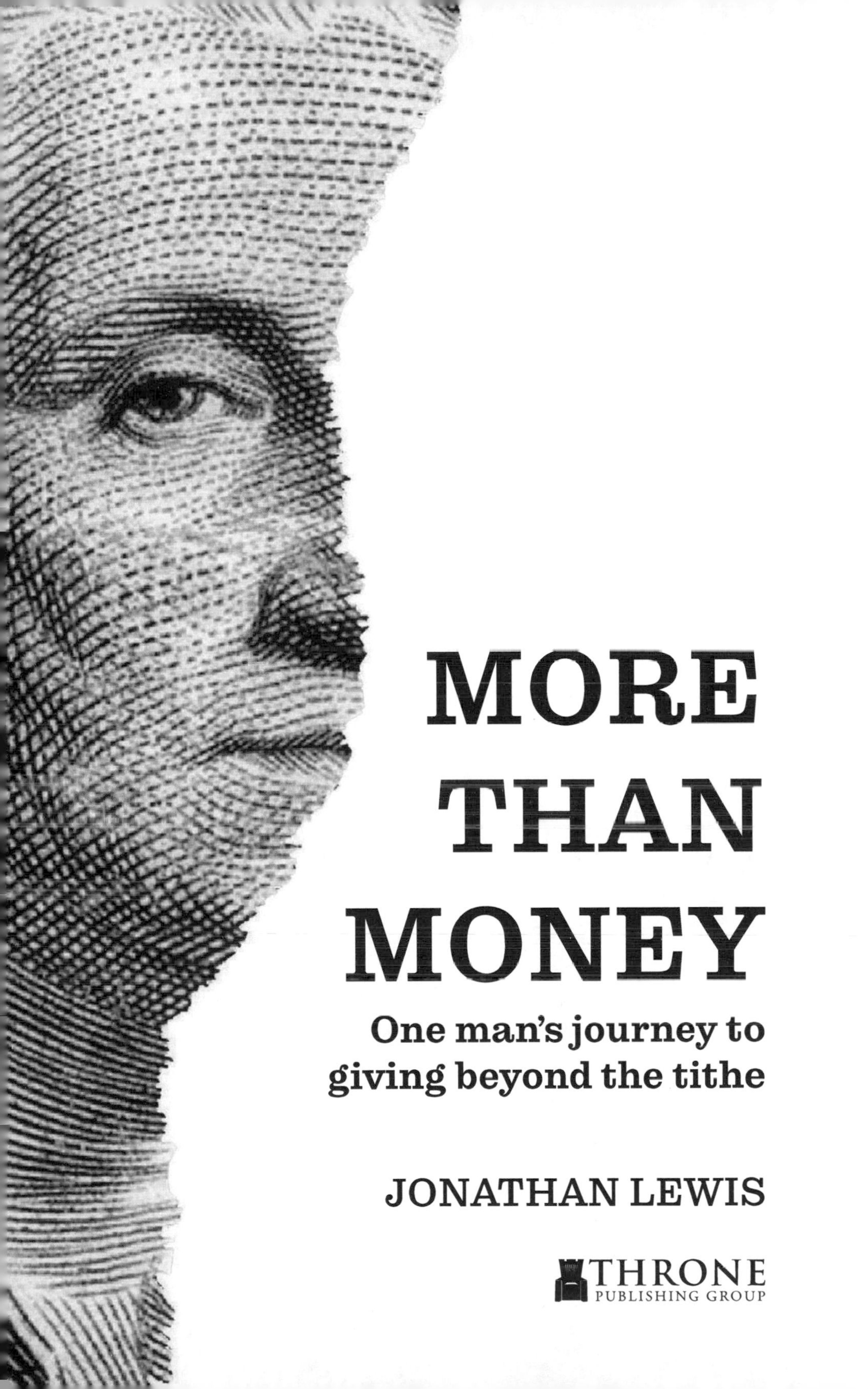

MORE THAN MONEY

One man's journey to giving beyond the tithe

JONATHAN LEWIS

THRONE
PUBLISHING GROUP

Hardcover ISBN: 978-1-949550-65-8
Softcover ISBN: 978-1-949550-52-8
Ebook ISBN: 978-1-949550-55-9

Printed in Canada.

Cover Design: Tim Murray
Interior Design: Heidi Caperton
Lead Writer: Paul Chaney
Editor: Marguerite Bonnett
Proofing Editors: Vicki Rich, Earl Menchhofer and Lucy Lee
Publishing Manager: Timothy Jacobs

Throne Publishing Group
1601 East 69th St N Suite 306
Sioux Falls, SD 57108
ThronePG.com

DEDICATION

Mark and Kim DeJager and Russell and Nancy Knowles,
Your influence in my life set the foundation for this book ten years later. If it wasn't for a few intimate, pivotal moments with you and your families, this book would not have been possible. My prayer is that it impacts many lives for eternity.

You have fulfilled scripture in my life and that of my family.

Thank You.

Psalm 68:5-6

ACKNOWLEDGMENTS

My Mom for instilling the truth of the Gospel of Jesus Christ into my heart as a young child.

Russell Knowles and Bruce Havill for introducing me to the currency of Heaven.

Kingdom Advisors Canada and US for all the amazing Biblical teaching that they provided me and the leadership team.

Sara, my wife, for coming along this amazing journey of faith with me.

TABLE OF CONTENTS

FOREWORD

As the National Director for Kingdom Advisors in Canada, a ministry to Christian financial professionals, I have become accustomed to receiving calls from different regions of the country. One such call was from Jonathan Lewis in the fall of 2017. He proceeded to ask some very probing questions to determine the credibility of this ministry and my own motives. However, I soon discovered that he was searching to find a deeper understanding of his own calling and purpose. He had a desire for all that God intended for him, but felt this was nearly impossible in his current role as a very successful financial advisor. He was struggling with exactly how to live out his calling and I felt an immediate alignment with my own journey.

I had started my career as a pastor, but in 2008, during the stock market crash, I was actually a seasoned financial advisor. This tumultuous time in the financial world caused me to question God's call on my life more than ever. During this season of deep soul-searching, I was transformed by my study of stewardship and the fact that God owns it all. Totally surrendering my practice to His ownership resulted in a profound sense of fulfillment as an advisor. However, the call to steward my other giftings and talents led me to make a major life decision to leave my 24-year career as an advisor and become "a pastor to financial advisors." A true understanding of stewardship helped me realize that I could have more of a kingdom impact by ministering to Christian financial professionals across Canada than I could have as an advisor. We are not all called to transition into new careers, but we all need to be transformed in our thinking to properly manage all that God has entrusted to us. I knew in my initial conversation with Jonathan that a proper understanding of stewardship would also affect him profoundly and set him on a journey that would impact others as well.

Scripture says, "the purpose in a man's heart is like deep water" and not easily discovered, but it is not impossible to "draw it out" (Prov. 20:5). Interestingly, Jonathan's first book about the impact of fatherlessness is entitled "Deep Water." This second book is a result of his intense searching and studying on the topic of stewardship. Jonathan quotes a favorite parable where Jesus told about a treasure that was hidden in a field. The parable does not reveal exactly what that treasure might be, but its discovery impacts the decisions being made. This treasure is buried; you have to search for it. Jonathan has discovered that the key to a more fulfilled life is becoming a better steward of all that God has entrusted to us.

Some may think that a book about stewardship by a financial advisor would simply focus on handling money. However, this book may surprise you because it will deepen your understanding beyond managing finances to areas of your life that you have not previously considered. Jonathan's zeal for stewarding life is evident in his writing. His transparency and personal story-telling are convicting, yet, refreshing and insightful.

When Jesus began proclaiming the good news, the instruction was to repent and believe. The word repent means to "rethink" and "live your life in a way that proves repentance" (Mark 1:15). That is exactly what this book challenges its readers to do and it will help you see the target of holistic stewardship more clearly. Once you see that prize, you will adjust your life as necessary to move toward that target.

LORNE ROBINSON
National Director - Canada
Kingdom Advisors

INTRODUCTION

> "For the time is coming when people will not endure sound teaching but having itching ears, they will accumulate for themselves teachers to suit their own passions and will turn away from listening to the truth and wander off into myths. As for you, always be sober-minded, endure suffering, do the work of an evangelist, fulfill your ministry" (2 Timothy 4:3-5).

I begin this book on stewardship by quoting Second Timothy because I believe it applies to the North American church in 2021, and I feel a need to raise an alarm. We are in such a willful or diluted state of disobedience with so much false teaching and self-worship that most Christians are no longer clear on the dividing line between the profane and holy, or if one even exists. We have become acclimated to the injustice of what we are doing or, more accurately, what we are not doing. We breathe in the air of prosperity in North America. In the meantime, Christianity is in a state of atrophy here while it flourishes elsewhere among the world's persecuted and poor.

In this book, I am going to wrestle with you, Dear Reader, about the same issues I struggled with regarding the true nature of biblical stewardship. I am also going to challenge you concerning the state of your heart towards God. Someone once said to me, "Jonathan, share your story. People may not like it, but it's awfully hard to argue with it because it's your story."

Some of what I have learned in my walk with God shared in the pages that follow will sting. It stung me when I started to grapple with what the Holy Spirit revealed about stewardship. Stay with me to the end, however. My prayer is that my story **will** sting, but in a good way.

MY INVITATION

This book is both a call to action and a repentance life in its fullest expression. Through holistic biblical stewardship, use of the resources we have been given, and empowerment by the Holy Spirit to glorify God and build His kingdom, we can live this Christian life. First and foremost, however, it is written to challenge you to answer a critical question, one that has bearing on eternity for you and those you love: **Who owns it all?**

David makes the ownership claim explicit in I Chronicles 29:11-12:

> Yours, LORD, is the greatness and the power and the glory and the majesty and the splendor, for everything in heaven and earth is yours. Yours, LORD, is the kingdom; you are exalted as head overall. Wealth and honor come from you; you are the ruler of all things. In your hands are strength and power to exalt and give strength to all.

Why is the ownership question so important? If you read God's Word, it is clear that stewardship is a cornerstone element in our growth as Christians. If we don't bear fruit, the outcome of stewardship, Jesus plainly states that we are not of His kingdom. If we are not His, we are serving someone or something else entirely. And if the church is not fulfilling the Great Commission, carrying the good news of salvation to the world, then it is hoarding resources for itself rather than sacrificing them for the Gospel's sake.

More than two thousand three hundred and fifty verses in the Bible talk about money and how God wants it used. In the Gospels, Jesus has more to say about money than heaven and hell combined.

I once heard Ron Blue, the Christian financial advisor, say, "Show me where you put your money, and I'll show you where your heart is." If we look at the average giving of the church, we have our answer. In 2020, the more than ninety million people in the U.S. and Canada who identified as evangelical Christians reported an aggregate income of over 8 trillion dollars. However, the average giving to the local church is just around 2.5%. You read that right: 2.5%. That means we are spending 97.5% percent on ourselves. Historically, giving in the U.S. was higher per capita during the great depression at 3.3% than it is today.

How are we, the wealthiest humans who have ever lived, going to respond when Jesus asks us to give an account as He did of those servants in the parable of the talents in Matthew 25? We are those servants. So, ask yourself, which am I? The servant who buried his talents or who stewarded them faithfully? Jesus' response to the unfaithful servant is clear: "Throw that worthless servant outside, into the darkness, where there will be weeping and gnashing of teeth."

The state of the church is dangerously close to that described in Second Timothy 3:1-5. Paul says we are lovers of ourselves who have a form of godliness but deny its power. We play church and build our castles while His house sits in ruin. It's time for the church to wake up. We are in danger of Jesus saying, I don't know you. "I never knew you."

There are consequences to our disobedience both now and in eternity. We rob ourselves of our walk with God and the spiritual growth that comes as a result. Not only do we grieve the Holy Spirit, depriving ourselves of His counsel and discernment, but we also fail to produce the fruit of the spirit: love, joy, peace, patience, kindness, goodness, gentleness, meekness, and self-control.

As human beings, we are hard-wired to live for ourselves — hedonism, the pursuit of pleasure, self-indulgence. But Jesus is calling us to be bond servants. However, He accompanies His command with two promises: "My Father will honor the one who serves me" (John 12:26) and "My yoke is easy, and my burden is light." (Matthew 11:30) We are in bondage one way or the other — either to a creator who loves and cares for us or to ourselves and Satan. In 1979, Bob Dylan sang about the devil, the Lord, and how you have to serve somebody.

As a Christian, think about your role in the world. Why did God put you here where you are now at this moment? What is His purpose for you? To simply serve yourself or commit your life and resources to Him unreservedly?

I would argue your sole purpose on earth is to glorify God. That's it! If that thought stings a little, perhaps it's because the Holy Spirit is convicting you of the idolatry of putting yourself first — "self" seated on the throne of your life rather than Christ. Consider this a wake-up and shake-up call. Do you want Jesus on your terms or His?

If that resonates with you, before reading another page, get on your knees, repent, and like the Chronicler, answer the question with this bold confession: "It's yours, Lord. It's all yours. I give it all to you — my life, resources, talent, treasure, family, and everything. Make me your bond servant and help me fulfill your purpose for my life, this day and every day until you call me home."

Time and time again, it's become evident to me that if you're serious about stewardship and growth in your relationship with Jesus, you have to be willing to go the distance. You have to be ready to storm the gates of heaven and not be cursory in your attempt. There's the "Old Harvard" try, and the "We tried but didn't really want to succeed" try. God says, "If you want to try me, then try me — it won't be me who quits on you. If you don't quit, I'll open the door and show you the path forward." (Luke 11:9-13)

I understand if you are reluctant. It isn't always pleasant at the time, but it will be powerful after the fact. You will be a different person — a better person, free from the love of money, need for control, jealousy, frustration, striving, or whatever else holds you back from complete devotion to Jesus. You will know your calling and where. You won't have to stare into a bowl of Cheerios praying for God to show you. If you demonstrate obedience with what He has entrusted you, He won't waste it. He WILL use you. You will walk with purpose and resolve. You will experience freedom from fear (one of Satan's primary weapons against you), pride, and selfish ambition.

In this book, we define biblical stewardship, discuss its importance to the believer, and examine its building blocks: money, of course, but also time, body, mind, energy, talent, creation, relationships, and grace.

My goal is that this book ignites a heartbeat of stewardship that causes you to step out courageously and follow Jesus wholeheartedly. It is also to help you understand that these building blocks are without merit unless they are energized by the Holy Spirit and matched with your particular spiritual gifts. Only then can you discern your unique calling and purpose in bearing fruit for the kingdom of God.

The adventure of stewardship in all areas of your life starts with the first step. Are you ready? Let's GO.

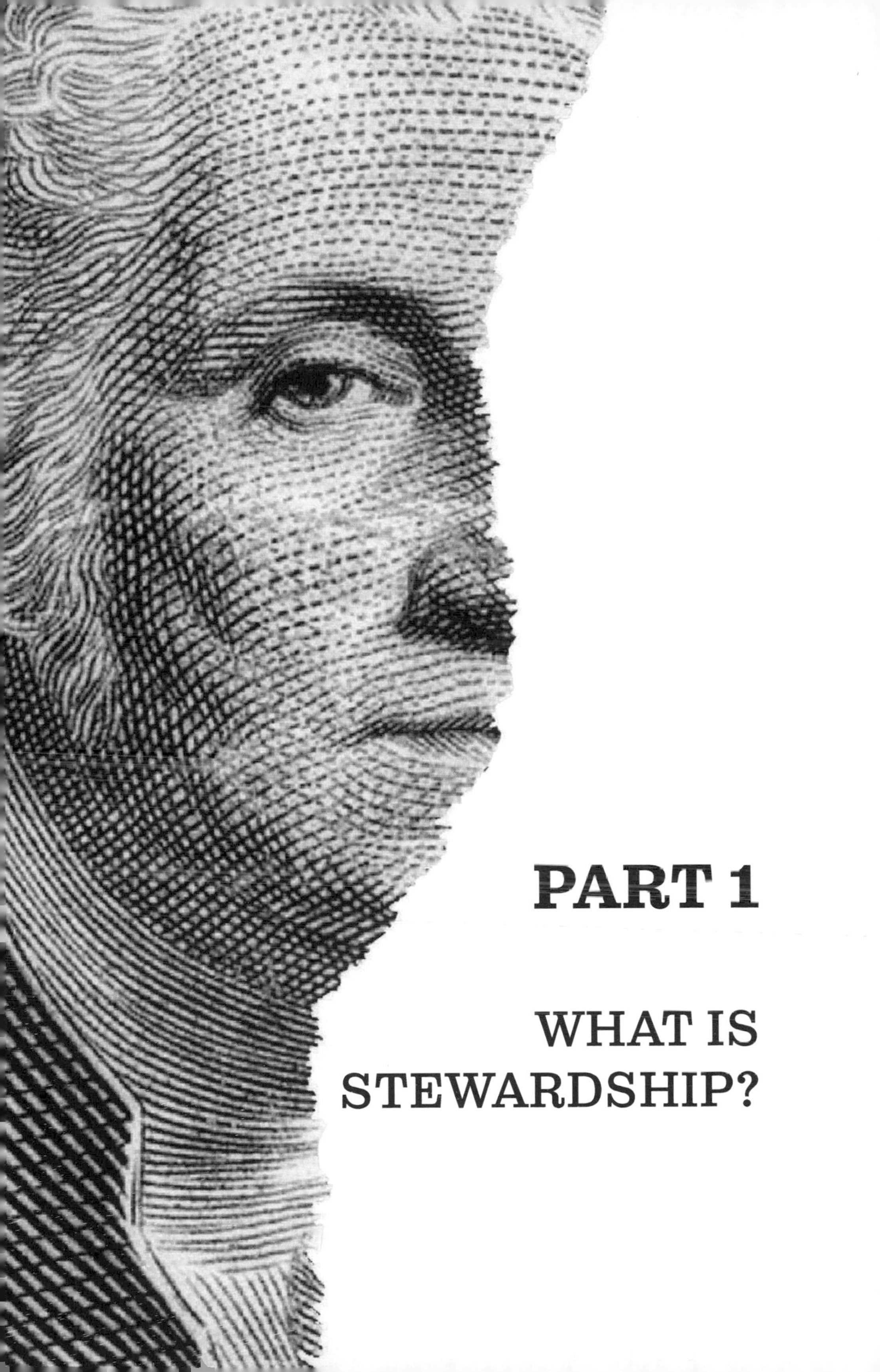

PART 1

WHAT IS STEWARDSHIP?

CHAPTER 1

Seeing the Prize

A story about a grandfather and his grandson sitting on a porch at the old man's farm on a warm summer's day resonated with me. The man had several dogs that made the fields surrounding the farm their home. As the grandfather sat with his grandson, chatting away, a slight breeze caused one of the dogs to spring from his slumber in the shade of the porch. He took off in a dash towards the tree line closest to the farmhouse across the field, howling with excitement, his nose pointed in the air. He had caught a rabbit's scent and had his eyes fixed on the creature in the grove ahead. Hearing the commotion, the other dogs jumped up and took off in close pursuit, howling and barking.

Seeing this, the grandfather looked at his grandson and said, "Son, do you see that dog tearing across the field ahead of the others?" His grandson nodded and said, "Yes, grandpa." The old man leaned in and said, "Son, let me tell ya what's about to happen. In about ten minutes, all but the first dog will come back with their tongues hanging out of their mouths, tired and thirsty, wanting a drink from that bowl of water on the ground there. Then, they will take their positions back under the shade of the porch. In about thirty minutes, that first dog will come back with a rabbit in his mouth. And son, do you want to know the difference between that first dog and the others? He's the only one who actually saw the rabbit. The others are just barking, simply wanting to be close to the excitement."

The lesson in this story is you need to *see* the thing that will ultimately sustain you in your pursuit of it. As we share and explore biblical stewardship in all its facets, my prayer is that you see the *prize* that is the reward for your efforts.

A favorite parable of mine is one Jesus shared in Matthew 13:44. It consists of a single verse yet is a powerful part of our journey towards seeing that prize. "The kingdom of heaven is like treasure hidden in a field, which a man found and covered up. Then in his joy, he goes and sells all that he has and buys that field."

For Christians, the prize is Jesus. The question is, do you see Him? Do you get what He did on the cross for you? If not, let me show you how.

Saved by Grace Alone

The British writer and lay theologian C.S. Lewis was once asked by his peers at Cambridge the difference between Christianity and all other religions. His response: "That's easy; it's grace."

Like all other religions, without grace, salvation would be something we need to earn and work to achieve by our own merits. Christianity is very different. We can't save ourselves from sin, greed, and self-destructive behavior, no matter how hard we try. It's God's grace and His grace alone that saves us. The greatest act of stewardship ever performed was modeled for us on the cross two thousand years ago. A debt was paid for you and me.

Through Jesus' death on the cross, we are pardoned for what we could never remediate ourselves. I think most Christians know this intellectually, but I wonder how many of us truly see the "rabbit," so to speak? We can't have that prize on our terms. We need to realize it on Christ's. To paraphrase Ephesians 2:8, it is by grace that we are freely forgiven, and by grace, we are called to freely give.

So, knowing it is by grace alone that we are saved and not our works, the question is, "Where do we go from here?"

A friend once said to me, "J, I think of myself as a beggar (when referring to himself as a sinner saved by the grace of God) who found bread showing other beggars where they can find bread, too. I'm a sinner saved by Jesus, no better than the next guy." It was a humble acknowledgment of who we are, apart from the amazing work done by Jesus on the cross: beggars lost in sin starving and decayed and wretched. The question is, "Do we *see* it?"

Fitting Jesus Into Our Box

In John's account of one of Jesus' first large public engagements, Jesus feeds five thousand people. Today, we know that number likely only included men; the actual figure was close to twenty-five thousand people, including women and children. After that fantastic miracle, Jesus withdrew by Himself to rest and gain reprieve from people who, according to John 6:15, sought to make Him their king.

People wanted to fit Jesus into their box right out of the gate. They had designs on what they wished Him to be to them. They thought He was a prophet; they desired a king who could deliver them from Roman rule. They liked His teaching, and they sure enjoyed His free food. Even in those early days, people wanted God on their terms. Sound familiar? We haven't changed much, have we?

Then, in the early morning hours, Jesus walks out to His disciples. Consider the fact they were in a boat… on the Sea of Galilee… in a storm, and you realize Jesus was walking on the water! What was He doing? Rescuing the disciples by calming the storm and their anxious hearts.

The following day, Jesus makes His way from Tiberias on the western shore of the Sea of Galilee to the north, in Capernaum, approximately sixteen kilometers or ten miles. The crowd has followed Him, and more have gathered on land and in boats. Then, Jesus shares with them why it is so important not to seek things that perish, like the food He fed them the day before, but food that "endures to eternal life."

Jesus tells the crowd in verse twenty-nine, "This is the work of God, that you believe in Him whom He has sent."

The dialogue continues. They question Him more on this eternal "bread" He referenced that God provides, and Jesus says in verse thirty-five, "I am the bread of life; whoever comes to me shall not hunger, and whoever believes in Me shall never thirst." He challenges their disbelief and tells them His calling (His purpose, if you will) from God: "Everyone who looks on the Son and believes in Him should have eternal life, and I will raise Him up on the last day."

The Jews now start to grumble and try and put Him in their

predefined earthly box. "He is just Jesus, the carpenter's son. He's come down from heaven? Come on!" Jesus persists. In verses forty-three through fifty-one, He says plainly, "I am the bread of life." He is laying it all on the table now. He's not going to be what they (or we) want Him to be. He is going to be who God sent Him to be. Period. Hard stop. By verse fifty-two, they are in all-out conflict among themselves. If that also sounds familiar, it's because that's the church today. We often want Jesus "a la carte."

I'm sure there were many in that sea of people who liked Jesus better when He fit into the box they had in mind for Him. But Jesus lays it on thick to the end of verse fifty-nine. Love it or leave it. I'm here for one purpose. He brings it home in verse sixty. When many of His disciples heard this — not the crowd but His actual followers — they asked, "This is a hard saying; who can listen to it?"

By verse sixty-six, those not granted spiritual understanding turned back and no longer walked with Him. Jesus then asked those who were left, "Do you want to go away as well?" Simon Peter quickly responds, making a statement that could only have come by divine revelation: "Lord, to whom shall we go? You have the words of eternal life, and we have believed, and have come to know, that you are the Holy One of God."

Wow! Now there is a guy who gets it. He saw the prize. At that moment, Peter has answered the question most of the western church has yet to. We still want Jesus on our terms, not His. I can't help but ask why. What are we hanging onto? The same thing the man Jesus encounters in Mark 10:17-27 — the rich young ruler.

This young man is eager to hear Jesus tell him what he can

do to inherit eternal life. We know how the interaction goes. In verse twenty-one, Jesus looks at him with love and tells him to sell all that he has, give it to the poor, and follow Him. In verse twenty-two, the young man goes away disheartened and sorrowful because he has great wealth. Jesus cut straight to the core of the issue, confronting him about his love of money and possessions instead of God. In doing so, Jesus gets to the heart of what stewardship is truly all about.

THE TAKEAWAY

We can't have Jesus on our terms. We must accept Him on His. That is the only path to salvation. It's not by our works but by His grace. The question is, "Do we see it?"

Explore the discussion questions on the following page.

Who is seated on the throne of your life? You or Jesus?

What are some ways people try to fit Jesus into their "box"?

What would it take for you to "see" Jesus as the "prize" worth pursuing? If you are a Christian, what did it take for you to accept Him as Savior?

CHAPTER 2

Stewardship: A Matter of the Heart

So how does stewardship fit into what I have just described? It forces us to go deeper with Christ. It separates those who, like Peter, "get it" from those who don't. Interestingly, stewardship is the only part of the Christian life that can't be counterfeited. You either go all in, or you try and fake it, institutionalize it, or fall away.

Jesus states in Matthew 6:21, "Where your treasure is, there your heart will be also." You could reverse that and say where a man's heart is, there lies his treasure. Stewardship is a heart issue, but stewardship in its fullest expression is not just about your "treasure" (i.e., your money). It's everything: your time, talents, mind, body, relationships, and all the other resources with which God has blessed you.

Neither is stewardship just giving ten percent in a church service on Sunday. It is a willingness to sacrifice whatever you have, in response to what Jesus Christ has done by offering Himself up entirely on the cross. It is a form of "heart surgery" that God uses to draw us into an intimate relationship where He can reveal Himself daily, allowing us to be a small part of what he is doing. As Proverbs 18:16 says, "A gift opens the way and ushers the giver into the presence of the great."

Stewardship is an action that reflects a profound understanding that everything we have belongs to God. We have lost something the moment we relegate stewardship to the tithe. Tithing is stewardship on training wheels when it comes to understanding, trusting, and giving back to God what is already His.

What God wants is a heart willing to sacrifice and find joy in doing it. He wants that "aha" moment Peter displayed in his revelatory statement. It's then that Jesus can work with us and in us to accomplish His purpose. Otherwise, we run the risk of becoming like the scribes and Pharisees. They legalized their faith and missed the point of giving altogether. Matthew 23:23 says, "Woe to you, scribes and Pharisees, hypocrites! For you tithe mint and dill and cumin and have neglected the weightier matters of the law: justice and mercy and faithfulness. These you ought to have done, without neglecting the others."

I once heard Kirk Cousins, quarterback of the NFL's Minnesota Vikings, say in a speech about giving he gave to a church group, "If we believe in what the Bible says and we trust God, why aren't we all in?" As we explore stewardship together, ask yourself, "Do I need some heart surgery on this, Lord? Have I acknowledged that it's all Yours? Am I living like it's all Yours, or am I just paying lip service, picking and choosing what I like about Your teaching? If so, what am I holding back out of all that You have entrusted me with and why?"

The theologian Carl F. Henry said, "The Gospel is only good news if it gets there in time for people to hear about it." Time is ticking down on the world, and God will hold us to account for what we did with what we are entrusted.

Diesel Fumes, Abundance, and Tears

The Apostle Paul said in Philippians 4:11, "Not that I am speaking of being in need, for I have learned in whatever situation I am to be content."

God used that verse to give me a much richer understanding of stewardship than what I had. Soon after I became a Christian, I volunteered to help build a new addition to a school and orphanage called Pueblo Nuevo run by a past coworker and friend, Mark, and his wife Kim, in an impoverished, rural Peruvian village named Ferreñafe, in the northeastern part of the country.

The night after arriving in Ferreñafe, I was invited to a prayer meeting and bible study in a church member's home with a small group from Nueva Vida. As I walked through the door into the host's home, I entered a room filled with an overpowering stench of diesel fuel that made my eyes water. The room, which I thought was a garage because it contained a motorcycle and tools and had a hard-packed clay floor, was actually the family's living room. After we left the meeting, Mark explained that the motorcycle was inside to keep it from being stolen. The family had spread diesel fuel on the floor to repel mosquitoes, a gesture of courtesy intended for my comfort and to welcome me as their guest. It was an act that came at great expense to the family, he said.

The family's humble dwelling consisted of clay or concrete

walls, a tin roof, and a dirt floor. They would be considered poor by first-world standards. Still, it didn't take me long to realize that while these people lacked the resources I had in abundance, they had an abundance of something I severely lacked. Their facial expressions and actions radiated contentment, joy, peace, and a sense of purpose that I did not have — intangibles money can't buy. They understood at a deep level what Jesus meant in Matthew 6:25 when He said not to worry because He will take care of our needs.

I remember feeling deeply moved and convicted as we drove back to where I was staying. The diesel fumes that had caused my eyes to water earlier quickly gave way to streams of tears. I had never felt so warmly welcomed in my life. I remember feeling deeply convicted. I knew I was among people of like spirit but still could not fathom how those who had little to nothing could show such love and hospitality to a total stranger.

Growing up in North America, I had no memory of experiencing anything like this. I lived in one of the wealthiest places on earth at a time when there is more prosperity than Solomon could have dreamed of. I found myself asking why was this new to me? What had I been missing until now? It was disturbing and, yet, exhilarating to think I was on the precipice of something new and extremely important. It was as if I found that treasure buried in the field the parable talks about.

Green Grass and a Swimming Pool

The people in Ferreñafe lived in a scorched, arid region where nothing grew other than during the short rainy season. The landscape was brown as far as the eye could see, with dust and sand blowing in all directions.

I had owned a landscaping company during university and knew I could grow grass anywhere. Mark was keen on giving the kids a place to play in front of the new schoolhouse, so I asked him to take me to the nearest hardware store — over an hour's drive one way into the city of Chiclayo — where I bought grass seed and other landscaping supplies.

With help from Mark and the rest of the kids at the school, we carved out an area about one hundred forty feet by sixty feet in front of the new schoolhouse that had just been built. We got to work prepping the ground and sowing the grass seed. The people had plenty of chickens, so we used the manure as fertilizer. We watered the newly planted lawn from the deep well at the center of the property, and I taught Mark how to maintain it once grass began to appear. Two weeks later, after returning home, he sent me a picture of a lush, green lawn.

During my time in Ferreñafe, I also realized that the school children had never been swimming due to the climate, nor had they ever been to the Peruvian coast and seen the ocean. While at the hardware store, I saw a small above-ground swimming pool. It wasn't fancy but was a pool nonetheless, so I bought it and loaded it in the truck. Back in Ferreñafe, we erected the pool and filled it with water. To this day, I have never seen a group of kids so happy! It was nearly impossible to keep them out of the pool until it was filled.

At the end of a long, hot day, when all the children finally headed home or to the dorms on the compound to get cleaned up for dinner, I looked at the pool. It was the dirtiest water I'd ever seen! But the smiles on the children's faces were the brightest

I had ever seen, too. I couldn't help but think how much of a metaphor that dirty water represented. How God meets us where we are, invites us to bathe in the clean waters He provides and sends us away with a new appreciation of the world as seen through His eyes.

A New Understanding of Stewardship

After the Peru experience, over the next five or six years, I poured through the Bible to learn all I could about stewardship. I read passages like Matthew 6:21, "For where your treasure is, there will your heart be also." I began to understand stewardship the way God intended, as expressed by the Peruvian people. They had shown tremendous grace and hospitality. Even with little, they gave with open hands.

I thought to myself, "If these people could do that with no material wealth, how much more was expected of me, a person with means? I have a world-class education, live in a prosperous, free nation, and have an excellent livelihood."

The Holy Spirit convicted and challenged me about my world-view. I realized what I had was not mine, that God owned it all. I was only a steward of what He had entrusted me with — my relationships, time, resources, talents, everything! It was also becoming abundantly clear that God expected results in return.

All I could think about was the parable of the talents in Matthew 25. I knew I would need to give an account, and, frankly, I wanted to get in the game and do my part. A longing grew in my heart to, one day, hear Jesus say, "Jonathan, well done, good and faithful servant." I knew I **didn't** want to hear Him say, "Jonathan, I showed you grace, and you squandered what I trusted you with. Away from me... I don't know you."

Reading scripture from a stewardship mindset and enlightened understanding of abundance was eye-opening. In North America, we think abundance equals money. There, in that little Peruvian village, far removed from the materialism that infects our culture — "affluenza" as I call it in my business — I realized for the first time that it had very little to do with money and much more to do with intangibles, like peace, contentment, joy, and daily walking with God. I grasped that stewardship is so much more than society's and, often, the church's narrow views. It is, instead, holistic, encompassing every aspect of our life. No wonder Jesus spent more time talking about this than He did heaven and hell combined.

Stewardship Lessons Learned

I took away several life-changing lessons from that trip. One of the biggest was that stewardship is communal, rooted in an abundance of grace for each other in the world we live in. When you steward what you have to meet each other's needs, it impacts both you and the entire community where God has placed you.

I also learned that stewardship isn't just about sharing what we can see and touch, money and possessions. It also consists of so many intangibles. In Ferreñafe, everything was exchanged:

- Time - the people made time to welcome me into their home and community;
- Faith - their mature faith was an inspiration;
- Wisdom - stewardship is about working with what you have, not getting more before you start;

- Energy - they volunteered to help build the schoolhouse and lawn;
- Relationships - people were investing in each other;
- Grace - God's grace was on display all the time.

The people had demonstrated stewardship in its fullest expression from the first time I set foot in their community. They gave out of their resources to buy diesel to spread on the floor and food for the gathering. As far as money goes, yes, I had more, but what they had went much deeper: a depth of faith and willingness to share as I had never seen or experienced.

That trip was pivotal for me, one I will never forget. It is a memorial stone that marks the moment when I realized, for the first time, what genuine biblical stewardship was all about, and where I witnessed, firsthand, the church engaging in its loving practice holistically.

PERU

THE TAKEAWAY

Stewardship is people who have a heart for Jesus coming together collectively and sharing what they have, in order to do good works, point people to Christ, and encourage each other in the process.

Ponder your thoughts on stewardship with the questions on the following page.

Based on this chapter, how would you define stewardship?

After reading the chapter, in what ways has your understanding of stewardship changed?

Are you stepping up in your faith with all God has entrusted you or are there areas where you are holding back? What actions do you need to take to go all in?

CHAPTER 3

My Journey to Understanding Stewardship

> "And without faith, it is impossible to please Him, for whoever would draw near to God must believe that He exists and that He rewards those who seek Him."
> —Hebrews 11:6

Christianity was part of my family's dialogue growing up. My mom was a strong believer who handed down her faith to her children by making sure we regularly attended church. On the other hand, my dad struggled with trusting God, even though he was the one who had introduced mom to Christianity in the first place.

Just after I turned fifteen years old, on a family outing by the sea, my dad died in a tragic SCUBA diving accident[1]. I blamed God — and myself — for Dad's accident. You see, I was with my dad in the water just offshore when he died, and despite my efforts to save him, I failed.

In my first book, *Deep Water: How to Face Fatherlessness, Fill the Gap, and Be the Man God Made You to Be*, I examine the void of fatherlessness and how to overcome it.

It took some time and a few years of struggle, but I finally and emphatically rejected whatever faith my parents had tried to instill in me. I simply could not reconcile where God was in this tragedy and how there was any truth in the promise that He cared for my family and me, given what happened to us after dad died. In the wake of my dad's death, I slowly lost hope. For the next nineteen years, I walked away in anger and frustration from what I knew to be true, that God loved me. Until, at the age of thirty-four, I found myself struggling in a troubled marriage, the father of two children under the age of two.

Something had to change. I was at the point of reconciliation with myself and God but didn't know how to sort through it all. I was suffering from PTSD, wasn't painful. I questioned that if I did, could I survive it emotionally. I just knew I was not happy and saw no way forward. My life was in shambles inside and out.

I started going back to church at that point. Someone had given me Rick Warren's book, *The Purpose-Driven Life*. There was a stirring in my spirit like I was searching for something but couldn't figure out just what it was. I was still resistant to the part God had to play and distinctly remember feeling very alone.

Planting Apple Trees and Hope

On a Sunday in July 2010, I planted some apple trees in the field next to my home. As I was digging holes to plant the trees, I stopped, sat down, and started to cry. I felt hopeless.

"Everyone wants the life I have except me," I sobbed. "It looks good on the outside, but the truth is I am lonely, and I hate the man I have grown to be. I hate who I am, who I've become, that my dad drowned and that I still feel responsible. I don't know how to come back from that. I have tried to do it myself for nineteen years, and I can't." Then, I looked up at a clear blue sky, paused, and said, "I don't know if you're there or not, Lord, but if you are, I need you to show up. I don't want to go it alone anymore."

The next morning, I was scheduled to meet a client for lunch at a restaurant near the hospital in the town close to where I lived. As it turned out, my client ended up canceling. Frankly, I was glad because I was too depressed to talk to anyone. I ordered lunch, then went to the bathroom to wash my hands.

When I returned, I found an older woman sitting in the booth opposite my place setting, where I had left my coat and a few personal items. She now had a place setting, and it was apparent she planned on staying. The restaurant was empty, which was unusual at lunchtime for this busy little spot so she could have sat anywhere. Plus, it was clear someone was sitting at the booth, and I thought, who sits in a booth that's clearly taken?

I admit to having some pretty hostile thoughts as I said to her, "I see you're sitting here, so I'll move to the next table." She replied, "I'm sorry. I didn't realize anyone was sitting here." She then relayed her story: "This is where my husband and I sat and ate lunch when we came to the hospital for his chemo treatments. It's hard to move on."

Her words hit a nerve. It had been nearly twenty years since my dad drowned, and I was stuck. "It is... really hard to move on," I said haltingly. She looked directly at me, my eyes locked with hers, and said, "You don't have to go to church for God to hear your prayer. He heard your prayer, and you're not alone." I had not told her (or anyone for that matter) anything about my marriage situation or otherwise. It shook me to the core.

Tears began rolling down my cheeks. I had always tried to put on a tough exterior, which, looking back, manifested itself in a lot of anger and frustration I could neither articulate nor reconcile. But now, I couldn't hold back. It felt like every ounce of pride was being stripped away, shed like a heavy winter coat, replaced with something more transparent and vulnerable. It was alarming. I felt exposed and didn't like it.

Thankfully, she shifted gears and talked about her marriage and all the years she and her husband had together, how it hadn't always been easy, but that they were committed to each other, relying on God to get through. Then she looked at me and said, "He wants you to fight for your marriage. He will honor that if you do."

"My marriage? Is she reading my mind?" I felt naked now. I wanted to run out of that restaurant, jump in my car, and drive as fast and far away as I could. But there was something about her compassion and grace, the kindness in her eyes, and the tone of her voice that made me feel safe.

We talked for an hour, and to this day, I can't decide whether she was an angel or a godly woman who was especially sensitive to the Holy Spirit. And I never even got her name! Either way, it was a seminal moment. That conversation was the start of my journey back to faith and another step toward understanding God and His character.

It was hard to convince myself that God would meet me where I was. I had spent almost two decades convincing myself He wasn't there and didn't care about my family or me. Could I, in my anger and brokenness, have walked away from the one who cared for me more than any other?

My Sincere Desire for Direction

As the summer of 2010 rolled on, I started to read the Bible for the first time in a long, long while. It became clear that finances were one part of my life, among many, that I needed to submit to God. At that moment, the concept of "stewardship" was a buzzword I vaguely understood as a child in church. I certainly had no comprehension that it intersected with every aspect of my life.

I intensely desired to know what God wanted me to do with my life and with all He had entrusted me: my talents, my time, my position in business, and my financial resources. I wanted to know why stewardship was important and how it impacts believers. It was profoundly clear even then that what I had was not mine but His. Yet it felt like a jigsaw puzzle with pieces spread all over the table and no instructions or picture to follow. So, I sought counsel from the pastors of the local church I was attending. I invited them to my office, spread out my financial statements, and asked bluntly, "What do I do?"

The poor men were dumbfounded. They didn't know how to respond. Looking back, I think during their combined years in ministry, they never had someone lay out their entire financial portfolio and ask, straight up, what to do with it. Even though they were genuinely willing to help, they simply were not equipped to provide the degree of knowledge and wisdom I was seeking. In their defense, they were younger than me, had little experience with affluent congregational members, and their teaching about stewardship didn't go much beyond the tithe.

Don't get me wrong. Tithing is a good starting point, and I wasn't even doing that. But I knew giving was the key that would break the chains of idolatry: my love of money, the world, and self. I had "money sickness" and needed to go deep with finding the cure.

Like so many, I was caught up in building my perfect little world, puffed up with pride, ignorant of anything beyond that. And why not? The world had taught me that "my self-worth was directly tied to my net worth." There I was, desperate to be free from the pursuit of what the world says our identity is rooted in. For the first time in my adult life, I was in fellowship with the Holy Spirit, and He was telling me that I didn't possess my money at all, but rather it possessed me. My money was spelled with a capital "M." That encounter was my first introduction to the local church's inability to train and equip believers in authentic biblical stewardship. Although I was looking for leadership regarding financial stewardship from the pastors, I quickly realized I would have to take ownership of this search if I was serious. I wasn't discouraged but was, instead, intent on pursuing God and understanding the nature of stewardship in every area of my life. Not getting answers proved to be a blessing. Because I had to work for it on my own, I received greater value as a result. Today, I know that experience was part of the Holy Spirit's plan to reveal my calling and purpose.

Years later, through Kingdom Advisors, a professional association for Christian financial advisors, I discovered teaching from men like Randy Alcorn, J.D. Greear, John Rinehart, Ron Blue, Ken Boa, Mitch Anthony, David Platt, Andy Stanley, Chip Ingram, and John Piper. My local church contributed to my education as well. Through it, I learned the truth of the Gospel, my responsibility, and what my response should be as a faithful steward.

Accepting the (Teen) Challenge

Rewinding to those formative years, my first exposure to Teen Challenge, a faith-based organization dedicated to helping youth battling substance addiction, occurred in 1988 at age thirteen. I attended a morning service at a church in New Jersey, not far from where Teen Challenge was birthed by David Wilkerson many years before, Times Square Church in New York City.

A group of Teen Challenge graduates had come from New York to share their stories about God's transformational power, freeing them from a life of drug addiction, violence, and abuse. As I sat and listened to their life stories, I realized, "This is the real deal. If God can do that for these guys, then nothing and no one is beyond Him." The experience left such a lasting impression that when a similar event took place at the local church I was attending with my daughters over twenty years later, I went! A group had come down from Teen Challenge locally, and I felt a deep connection. A long, almost dormant flame started to flicker a little brighter.

Wanting to be more involved, I pledged to support a young man to attend Teen Challenge in Canada annually. I also got to know Spenser Mason, the development officer from the local center. He had been an addict and, today is a youth pastor at a nearby church. I asked what I could do to help, and he told me to come to the center for a visit. I agreed to take him up on his offer. I promised to buy some steaks and all the fixings to go with it, and along with some friends, cook up a feast for the TC gang on a Saturday in early March a few weeks later.

I was still having marriage difficulties. A few days before we were to leave, I received more discouraging news that made me so despondent I did not want to go. I couldn't sleep. All I could think about was my children growing up in a broken home and how this simply wasn't what I wanted for them. I knew how deep the wounds were for me losing my dad, and I was desperate for my kids not to experience the same thing. I was down for the count and certainly didn't want to be around other people, let alone drive to Teen Challenge to try and lift anyone else's spirits.

When that Saturday morning rolled around a few days later, my friend Andrew challenged me. "It's not about you, Lewis; it's about them," He said. "You have to push through and follow through with what you said you would do for these guys. How much worse would it be for them if we promised to drive up and don't take the time." Andrew was right, of course.

That was enough to get me past my pity party. We hopped in the brand-new car I had just bought, drove to Costco, and loaded up twelve hundred dollars' worth of groceries — steaks, apple pie, bread, salad, dressing — everything needed for a three-course meal for a bunch of hungry men. The car was packed! My friends and I hit the road, two hundred and sixty miles (four hundred two kilometers) to the Teen Challenge center, a four-hour drive. The center is on a peninsula, surrounded by the Memramcook River in New Brunswick on one side and the Bay of Fundy on the other. (The Bay of Fundy boasts the world's highest tides, more than fifty feet. Google it. It will blow your mind.)

I know *now* that it is very common for the spring thaw, coupled with those crazy tides, to cause severe flooding in the area. We had no idea what we were in for at the time, however. Although the primary road was passable and the GPS told us to go one way, we accidentally took a wrong turn and found ourselves confronted with a real problem. Of course, when I say we *accidentally* took a wrong turn, what I *really* mean is a car full of men didn't trust the GPS. We crossed a road flooded from the spring ice blocks and tides off the bay, convinced we were going the right way. Ladies, you can say it. Men, you know it's true. Even with a device telling us the way, we knew better.

Common sense would dictate that driving through saltwater with ice and debris floating by when it's minus twenty-five degrees Fahrenheit in the dead of winter offers many terrible potential outcomes. But not realizing we had gone the wrong way, thinking this was the only route to get to the center, we drove onto the flooded road.

What we assumed would be just a little water and ice suddenly got much worse. Water began cascading over the windshield, and I couldn't see anything. One of my buddies, Andy, stuck his head through the sunroof to give me directions. "Punch it!" Andy yelled; so, I floored it, and we pushed through, barely making it to the other side. The car was chugging; it had taken in brackish saltwater through the air intake. "Not good," I thought to myself. "I wonder if this will be covered under warranty?" I pictured how the conversation at the dealership would go. "Oh yeah, it's really weird. The horn also doesn't seem to work now either. I guess I got a lemon."

After we crossed and pavement gave way to a dirt road, it finally dawned on us that we had gone in the wrong direction. Our hearts sank when we realized we would have to turn around and go back across the flooded road — but go back we did. We reached the center and had the time of our lives hanging out with the guys, cooking steaks, holding chapel, and praying for each other. What seemed, at the moment, like something I had no energy for turned out to be such a blessing for me personally, my friends, and those guys at Teen Challenge.

Through this time at the center, I encountered how God can show up and give us joy, a fruit of the spirit, even in our darkest hours. I was starting to realize that giving is something powerful. It breaks chains. Be it the turkeys we handed out a few months before for Christmas in 2010 (our first year doing it) or my trip to Peru a few weeks after that or this trip to Teen Challenge, I saw a pattern: No matter how bad things were in my life, my spirit and the spirit of others was lifted when serving God, serving others, and putting "self" aside.

Fast-forward ten years later. I'm now on the national board for Teen Challenge, Ambassador for Teen Challenge Atlantic in Canada, do countless events throughout Canada, and still go up to the center to cook steaks.

TEEN CHALLENGE

THE TAKEAWAY

Everyone has a journey, and, for many, it's not easy — not unlike crossing a flooded road. But it's all about attitude. If you focus only on your needs with a "What can I get?" attitude, not a "What can I give?" you are missing the point entirely.

Stewardship involves the act of giving, selflessness, and sacrifice in whatever area: time, talent, treasure, and more. That is where God meets you, restores and builds, and brings people together in community. It is what Jesus modeled for us when He freely gave His life and, in turn, the Holy Spirit. If it was good enough for Jesus to give what was His then, surely, it's good enough for us to give back to Him what is also His now.

In what ways has God revealed Himself to you? What was happening in your life at the time? Were the circumstances good or bad?

Describe a time when God revealed to you something had to change. What did you do to make that happen? How did you pursue Him? How did He show up?

Think about a sacrifice you made on behalf of others. How did it make you feel? In what ways did it benefit those you were trying to help? How did you benefit?

CHAPTER 4

Stewardship's Importance and Characteristics

Before we go any further, I want to explore with you the importance and characteristics of stewardship. God has a purpose for your life and understanding stewardship's importance and characteristics are fundamental to its fulfillment. He wants you to put "skin in the game," to place a bet on the table of life using His resources and let it ride.

The theologian John Piper said, "You just have to know a few basic, simple, glorious, majestic, obvious, unchanging, eternal things and be gripped by them and be willing to lay down your life for them." With that in mind, let's explore what God wants to *grip* us with regarding stewardship's importance and characteristics.

Perhaps you can tell that early on in my Christian walk, I was eager to go to bat for Jesus and grow in my faith, sharing who He is and what He did for me with those I encountered.

> **"DON'T TELL ME WHERE YOUR PRIORITIES ARE. SHOW ME WHERE YOU SPEND YOUR MONEY AND I'LL TELL YOU WHAT THEY ARE."**
>
> **—JAMES W. FRICK**

Jesus demonstrated His own stewardship by submitting to God and giving His life for us. I wanted to be a useful part of whatever He was doing in the world. I felt I had lots of gifts and talents that I had squandered on selfish pursuits, and I wanted to re-apply them to whatever God's purpose was for me.

My spirit was willing, and I felt like a racehorse who, for the first time, had an inkling of the race I was meant to run. I would stare into my bowl of Cheerios each morning, praying God would reveal His calling to me. I felt trapped in my career. I kept thinking maybe I'm supposed to sell everything and move to Guatemala and be a missionary or something. The problem was the only thing that my Cheerios ever spelled was "OOOOOOO."

I was confused, stuck in a world I had made for myself. I was a single dad, living in a town that I wasn't from, going to a church where I didn't fit. In short, I was caught between the old and the new. I believed in and accepted what Jesus did for me on the cross. I realized I was, as Paul says in Ephesians 2:8, saved by grace through faith, and I certainly knew I was a new man in Him.

But the old me didn't die easily. I was still straddling the world I left and this seemingly lonelier world I wanted to move toward called Christianity. It was messy. I didn't come to the church pre-sanctified. The flesh and the spirit were warring inside me. I didn't do any of the things I used to, nor did I hang out with a lot of my old friends, but I became withdrawn, using my divorce as an excuse.

I was still learning a lot of the basics and made many mistakes early on. I certainly wasn't ready to save the world. I needed training and coaching. I'm not even sure I'm prepared to "save" the world today, ten years later, but I do feel a clear calling and sense of purpose, and I'm certainly clear on who I am in Him. As such, I'm also clear on the part I am to play. My simple role is to glorify Him, point people to His son, and, when necessary, use words to paraphrase St. Francis of Assisi, "He will do the rest."

Stewardship and Justice

Stewardship and justice go hand and hand. In Micah 6:8, God commands the believer to "Do justice, love kindness, and walk humbly with your God."

The Old Testament says more than two hundred times that it is unjust for those in places of position and privilege not to leverage their influence on behalf of those without it. In God's eyes, justice is required. To not pursue justice is to disobey God willfully.

Matthew 23:23 is one good example of what Jesus considered justice and mercy and His contempt for those that withheld it.

Jesus says, "Woe to you, scribes and Pharisees, hypocrites! You pay a tenth of mint, dill, and cumin, and yet you have neglected the more important matters of the law — justice, mercy, and faithfulness."

We are not to turn our back on the poor, but to feed those in need, offer them shelter, and stand in the gap for widows and orphans. If we don't, we aren't His followers.

What "The Karate Kid" Teaches Us About Stewardship

I was having lunch with a friend with whom I had a part to play in leading him to Christ. We talked about the importance of stewarding our gifts and talents in the context of discerning our calling. He shared that he wished he knew what God's calling was for him.

As he talked, I felt the Holy Spirit saying, "I can't use you if you aren't equipped and prepared to do the work." I shared that with him. Then, I felt the Spirit saying, "If you won't do the little things that I ask you to do, how can I trust you with more?"

I know this will sound crazy, but I suddenly had a flashback to the *Karate Kid* scene where Mr. Miyagi is teaching Daniel LaRusso to "wax on, wax off," and I shared that with my friend. He laughed and we joked about how the Holy Spirit had distilled stewardship and knowing our calling down to *The Karate Kid*. However, it made sense to me, given we were a pair of middle-aged guys who grew up in the eighties.

If you saw the movie, you'll remember that Mr. Miyagi says he will teach Daniel karate and that he needs to come at six the next morning. When Daniel arrives, Miyagi puts him to work waxing all of his cars using a very specific technique, broad circular strokes, where he puts the wax on in one stroke and then takes the wax off with another.

The next day Miyagi makes poor Daniel "sand'a da floor" using similar but reverse motions. He sands all of Miyagi's decks and patios. The day after, Daniel paints the fence with a different motion. We all remember Miyagi walking away, saying loudly, "Up. Down. Up. Down."

Finally, when Daniel got frustrated with another day of the "side-to-side" painting of Miyagi's house, demanding to learn when he was going to teach him karate, Miyagi calls Daniel to attention. It's at this moment this brash young student discovers that all those motions, repeated for hours on end, were for a purpose.

Mr. Miyagi attacks, and Daniel instinctively defends himself by using the muscle memory of waxing the car, sanding the floor, painting the fence, and so on. Miyagi bows, says, "Come back tomorrow," and walks away. We know the rest of the story — Daniel returns, humbled, to learn more.

You might ask, how does this parallel our development as believers regarding stewardship?

Like Mr. Miyagi, God knows we are eager and willing, but He needs to develop us into mature spiritual believers. He knows that before He can use us for bigger things, we need to handle the smaller responsibilities He puts before us. He wants to see if we will do the work.

Are we committed, or will we be choked off like in the parable of the sower? (Matthew, 13:1-23, Mark 4:1-20, Luke 8:4-15) Will the world get the better of us? Will we let go of our pride and greed? Will we dive into His Word and not become discouraged? Will the seed planted in our hearts take root? He gave us free will. It's up to us to do the work and show we really want to *know* His will. Otherwise, the only word the bowl of Cheerios will ever spell is "OOOOO."

God's calling on our lives is the *what*. We know we are called to share the good news of the Gospel. The *why* is spelled out in Matthew 9:37, "The harvest is plentiful, but the laborers are few." The *how* is the union of the Holy Spirit and your willing spirit that, like the prophet Isaiah, says, "Here am I, send me Lord." (Isaiah 6:8) The *where* and *when* will become self-evident just like it was for Daniel LaRusso. We simply need to show up every day and work at what He gives us for that day.

That said, before we delve into this book any further, I want to clear up some misunderstandings that most Christians have about the nature of stewardship, what it is and is not. Let's start with the "not" part first.

What Stewardship Is Not

Stewardship is not hoarding God's resources. It's not prideful. It doesn't point people to you; it points people to Jesus. It doesn't envy others' work or efforts. Neither is stewardship about asceticism, giving up all your worldly possessions and living a life of self-denial, portraying the appearance of wisdom and humility. This can just as easily lead to religious pride as the man who gives out of His abundance for all to see. (ref. Colossians 2:20-23)

Martin Luther once said, "Satan doesn't care which side of the horse you fall off; he just wants to get you off the horse." Religious pride wrapped in asceticism is still sowing to the flesh as much as materialism.

Stewardship isn't about giving begrudgingly — "I can't afford it. We don't have a budget for it." It's about God wrestling with us in our hearts and breaking the bondage of whatever we're clinging to that prevents us from getting closer to Him. Jesus doesn't want us to give for His benefit but ours.

It's also not about the prosperity doctrine of giving to get. When you commit to true biblical stewardship, God will provide you with things you can't buy, like contentment, peace, joy, the fruit of the Spirit. But the only way to receive them is to push aside your pride and ego.

The problem is that we want everything to come so easily. But this isn't a one-and-done, twenty-one-day cleanse, or "Try God for a limited time offer, three easy payments of $9.99." Biblical stewardship takes real resolve. It's not wrapped in a religious blanket, and you can't just check boxes. It's a relational overhaul of your heart around whatever or whoever it is you're clinging to and don't have enough of.

The Bible would argue that it is impossible to be a follower of Christ and hold back what is His. In Malachi 3:6-15 — the same place we often point to when discussing the tithe — it says we are stealing from Him when we do.

Everyone Has a Price

If stewardship is having an open hand, freely giving what belongs to God to the world for His purpose and glory, the opposite is keeping it for ourselves. Satan's premise in this area of the battle for our souls is to keep encouraging us to crave, chase after, and acquire more. More money and more stuff. More trips and more toys. More friends and more "likes" on social media. Anything to feed the idol of self.

Early on in his reign, King Solomon was granted wisdom from God on account of his righteousness. Later, he grew greedy and, in his lust for more wealth, disobeyed God by amassing more horses, gold, silver, and wives than God told him to. (Deuteronomy 17:16-17) The things we cling to give us a false sense of security. We can look at Solomon and ponder what he was thinking. But, today, in North America, many of us enjoy much more splendor than Solomon could have ever imagined. What are **we** thinking?

"Everyone has a price" is what Satan is saying, and he is buying. What's your price? Judas's was a mere thirty pieces of silver. What matters isn't how much he betrayed Jesus for; it's what his heart was willing to do — for a price. The issue of Judas's heart was that he couldn't see where real eternal value resided. He could only see what he wanted as an outcome and when Jesus didn't fit his designs, he balked. He wavered, caved in, and sold his soul. The price was irrelevant.

Let me share an example — and I do this with reservation given its nature, but it drives the point home nicely. A billionaire at a party approaches a woman and offers her one million dollars to sleep with him. She accepts. As they leave the party together, he asks the woman, "Would you sleep with me for one hundred thousand dollars?" The woman stops and objects to the insult, asking, "What do you think I am?" He responds, "We have established what you are; now we are simply trying to determine your price."

I know this may seem a crude example, but the fact is mankind's heart has been sold out for money and other idols. We have been guilty of prostituting ourselves for it since the very beginning of time.

Israel, God's chosen people, would stray, following idols. Of them, the prophets would say, "My people ask counsel at their wooden idols, and their staff informs them. For the spirit of harlotry has caused them to stray, and they have played the harlot against their God." (Hosea 4:12) In Ezekiel 14 and, later in chapter 16, the prophet talks about how the people of Israel embraced idols and God's response — judgment and punishment for their sins. The lesson is that the moment we are willing to trade our soul for this world's things, the price becomes irrelevant.

It's worth noting that we are spiritual beings made in the image of God, and we will never be able to fill that void with non-spiritual things no matter how hard we try. I came to a place where it dawned on me that it is folly and a waste of time to chase after something like sand, having no transcendent value.

John D. Rockefeller once said, "The poorest man I know is the man who has nothing but money." Rockefeller, who died in 1937 as one of the wealthiest Americans who had ever lived, was a devout Christian who gave approximately one hundred thirty-eight million dollars to God's work. When asked how much he left in his estate, Rockefeller's accountant said, "All of it." Rockefeller understood Ecclesiastes 5:15 well: "Naked a man comes from his mother's womb, and as he comes, so he departs. He takes nothing from his labor that he can carry in his hand."

James 1:23 says, "Be doers of the word and not just hearers." In chapter 2:21-24, James recounts Abraham's obedience to God regarding offering his son Isaac on the altar. He sums it up in verse twenty-six by saying, "For as the body without the spirit is dead, so faith without works is dead also." Such is the character of stewardship.

What Stewardship Is

We examined in some detail what stewardship is not, so let's flip the coin and look at what it is.

Stewardship is:

- when we show God that He can trust us with what He gave us by working alongside Him diligently seeking His will.
- surrendering to Him and following Him on His terms, not our own, taking His Word in its entirety as divinely inspired.
- humbly, pointing people to Jesus and not us.
- fighting for God's justice in an unjust world. Not social or political justice but God's justice. As such, it is a critical part of Christian life.
- about examining the state of your heart and asking, "Am I willing to give of my time, talents, and treasure for the sake of the Gospel?"
- a response of the heart to what Jesus has done for **<u>you</u>**.
- acknowledging and answering the questions: Who owns it and who owns me? Whom do I serve, myself or someone more transcendent? Jesus or man. Do I truly understand the great act of stewardship He performed on the cross, and do I want to share that with the world?
- taking risks, taking action, and showing results. Psalm 119:105 says, "Your word is a lamp to my feet and a light to my path." There is no need for a light or path if you aren't going anywhere.

Stewardship Champions

The 'Anonymous Brothers'

One of the things I love most about stories on stewardship is the anonymity of those who step out for God's glory. We see the results but never know *who* was behind them. That's because in God's kingdom, "He" is the who, not us. Let me give you an example.

The brothers in Acts did a lot, but I bet you don't know who I'm talking about. It's right there in Acts. The "brothers" planted the churches in Antioch, Alexandria, and Rome. (Yes, Rome, before Paul even got there.) We have no idea who actually planted those three churches. Acts 11 simply says, "some brothers showed up full of the Spirit and planted a church." I love it. "Some brothers filled with the Spirit." Isn't that awesome? Paul spends the entire second half of Acts trying to get to Rome. His letter to the church in Rome got there before he did. When he finally arrives, the "brothers" have a thriving church already waiting for him. When he arrives, he discovers the "brothers" have already set up a church! Regular guys... filled with the Spirit.

Humphrey Monmouth

Humphrey Monmouth, someone most people in the church have never heard of, is a personal hero. I love his story because he was a businessman who took risks for God's kingdom.

Monmouth was an English cloth and textile merchant in London circa the early 1500s. Most people don't know that he is the man who funded the undertaking of the first Bible translation into English by William Tyndale, which was considered heresy at the time.

Monmouth was converted to the cause of reforming the church under the early ministry of Tyndale after hearing him preach one Sunday in London. Being an extremely wealthy man, Monmouth took Tyndale under his wing to live with him and fund his efforts. This was a deliberate and conscious choice to accept the risk that could lead not only to the loss of his entire business — a prosperous cloth and textile empire supported by a gigantic fleet of ships that spanned the English empire — but also his life.

Tyndale's translation reached every corner of the empire, smuggled inside rolls of cloth or vats of molasses in Monmouth's ships. The translation's spread was unstoppable because the merchant used his resources for the glory of God.

King Henry VIII tried to stamp out the influence of Tyndale's translation by burning him at the stake. Still, he was unable to due to the sheer number of Monmouth's ships, each of which carried the precious document.

As Tyndale was dying, his very flesh on fire, with his last breath, he cried out that the king's eyes would be opened. Monmouth was also imprisoned for a year for twenty-five criminal counts, including supporting Tyndale. He had a family, including two daughters, and a business that was now under attack. He had put "skin in the game" and risked what he had for something greater than his possessions or stature in society.

Monmouth passed away just ten months after Tyndale's death. Two years after the two men went on to stand before Jesus, their mission complete, the King of England ordered that an English Bible be put in every parish in the entire British Empire. The King's eyes had been opened by the testimony of Tyndale and his patron Monmouth.

Monmouth risked it all, and the result is four hundred years of an English translation of the Bible, which fueled the Reformation. Now I ask you, if you were one of the wealthiest men alive today, would you be prepared to risk it all? Are you, like Humphrey Monmouth, ready to risk what God has entrusted to you? There was no earthly incentive for him to take such a risk, only an eternal one.

Put Some Stewardship 'Skin in the Game'

I have used the term "skin in the game" a couple of times in the book. What I mean is that in the business world, a person who is investing in something can't easily walk away and just "set it and forget it." Successful business ventures require investors to bring their talents, skills, wisdoms, and experiences to bear. The investments usually make them vested in the entire process.

The businessperson is taking a risk. Failure often comes with terrible consequences. You can't be in halfway. I always say to myself when facing tough and risky choices, "One for the money, two for the show, three to get ready… and, yes, four to go!" But I see many Christians often sitting on the starting block still saying, "three to get ready… three to get ready." Umm, hello — GO!

Moneyball, starring Brad Pitt, is one of my favorite movies. In the film, Pitt's character, Billy Beane, has to decide whether he believes the system they were using to develop a winning ball club will work. Risking it all, refusing to cave to the pressure and play it safe, he doubles down and lets a bunch of players go, committing to the end game for better or worse. Everything was hanging in the balance — his career, reputation, and ability to stay in his daughter's life and provide for her — EVERYTHING!

Why is it that, as Christians, we cave at the moment of truth? Why don't we press in and go for it? I think it's because we don't genuinely believe God will show up. We cling to the illusion that we are in control.

Like Billy Beane and the business world, we need to decide to put skin in the stewardship game. Are we prepared to risk it all? Are we going to take God at His word when He says in Malachi 3:10, test me and see? Are we all in, prepared to be good stewards of what we have received from God, investing time, talent, and more, pursuing wise counsel? Right now, for most Christians, the mindset is, "Here's my ten percent" or, worse, nothing at all. "Do I still have a seat at the table?" instead of, "It's all yours, Lord, and I trust you."

That's the way it should be. But in the church, we often associate stewardship with fulfilling a religious mandate to give ten percent. We have done our sacred duty. We don't get involved. We give and forget. In that scenario, two people lose out. The giver loses because they are not going deeper in their stewardship journey and walk with Christ, but they also rob others who may lack the wisdom to use the gift.

Instead, we need to put skin in the game and say to struggling ministries, "Here's what you need, but I'm not going to just give it and walk away. I'm going to come alongside you and provide counsel and wisdom in its use so that it won't be squandered. And I'm going to give more in every way I can."

Like Billy Beane, we need to work together to ensure the gift is used to its full potential. Chasing the things of this world Monday to Saturday and heading off to church on Sunday isn't putting skin in the game. We may think we're fooling God; but, we're not. We are the ones who are deceived if we spend our time sowing ninety percent for ourselves and ten percent for God. Instead of skin *in* the game, we have merely secured an option to attend the game, and only if it suits us.

THE TAKEAWAY

Understanding stewardship's importance and characteristics are fundamental to knowing and fulfilling God's calling on your life. Otherwise, you will spend your time, like Daniel LaRusso, "waxing on and off" never realizing your full potential.

What does it mean to you to get a “grip” on stewardship?

Name three characteristics of stewardship.

Can you say with confidence that you have stewardship “skin in the game”?

CHAPTER 5

Stewardship Doesn't Go Unnoticed
The Principle of Sowing and Reaping

"Do not be deceived: God is not mocked, for whatever one sows, that will he also reap. The one who sows to his own flesh will from the flesh reap corruption, but the one who sows to the Spirit will from the Spirit reap eternal life."
—Galatians 6:7-10

"As for what was sown on good soil, this is the one who hears the word and understands it. He indeed bears fruit and yields, in one case a hundredfold, in another sixty, and in another thirty."—Mathew 13:23

Many great church leaders have taught God's principle of sowing and reaping: Dr. Charles Stanley, his son Andy Stanley, Dr. David Jeremiah, Bill Bright, and Billy Graham, to name a few.

I won't pretend to be an authority on this subject, but I definitely can see how this has shown up in my life in both good and bad ways. When the Bible talks about "sowing," it is in the context of a metaphor for planting, sowing seeds into the soil. The premise is we sow seeds; they germinate and sprout, ultimately bringing a harvest. The question for us is, what are we sowing? We can either sow weeds or good seeds that will bear good fruit, as the Bible puts it.

In God's universe, everything has action and reaction. Science supports that, and certainly, the Bible testifies to it. We can sow into our lives a generous heart that gives all we have to God, the basis for this book, and reap his reward.

Often, His reward is not what we want or more of what we gave, but what we need. For example, we may give money, and, in return, He gives us contentment and peace with what we have, not more money. He frees us from the love of money to pursue His will for our lives. Or we give our time to someone in need, and He blesses our business, knowing we took time away from it to serve Him. In either case, it is an amazing interaction of faith where He has the opportunity to show up time and time again in ways we could never imagine.

On numerous occasions, I have invested my time in someone dealing with a rough patch in their life only to discover that while I was quietly anxious about all the spinning plates in my life, God had my back on the work and home front.

It is liberating to sow and reap with God and is part of the journey of faith and sanctification we are all on. He gives us the fruit of the Spirit — love, joy, peace, patience, kindness, goodness, gentleness, meekness, and self-control — characteristics we can't manufacture or buy. (Galatians 5:22-23)

They have imposters that the world wants to sell us, of course: happiness in exchange for joy, for instance. But happiness is temporary and subject to external circumstances. The moment things aren't what we thought they were or that person doesn't please us like they once did, happiness evaporates. On the other hand, joy is internal and springs from within regardless of circumstances or people.

Mankind will chase endlessly after things, experiences, relationships, and all forms of pursuits to fill the hole in their lives. But we are spiritual beings, made in the image of God. To quote the French philosopher and theologian Blaise Paschal, "There is a God-shaped vacuum in the heart of each man, which cannot be satisfied by any created thing but only by God the Creator, made known through Jesus Christ."

If we sow into and pursue His kingdom, it will come. It takes time for reaping to occur, but it does come to pass. That is why Jesus said in Matthew 6:33, "But seek first the Kingdom of God and His righteousness, and all these things will be added to you." The "things" He is referring to are not material. It is what those people in Peru had that I was missing, the fruit of the Spirit, peace that passes all understanding, that there is a God who truly cares for you and me. You don't need to strive to survive in His kingdom. You simply need to lay down your burdens and sow the seeds He has given you and let Him weave you into His bigger tapestry of heaven.

The same is true if we sow to our flesh, which, if we're honest, is our default position. We go after the things we want and not what He prescribes for us. In doing so, we reap the consequences.

David Reaps the Whirlwind

The story of David and Bathsheba illustrates this principle so vividly. The Bible says that David was a man after God's own heart. But he was also fallible and lusted after another man's wife.

In 2 Samuel 11, when he should have been off to war, according to verse one, David takes a stroll one evening on the palace rooftop. He gets an eye full of Bathsheba as she bathes. By verse four, he has slept with her, and by verse five, she is pregnant. Holy smokes! David didn't waste time. In a few opening verses, the guy has, quite literally, sown the wind and is now reaping the whirlwind. But that's not all! He then has Bathsheba's husband, a good friend of his, killed and takes her as his wife to cover it up. Let the sowing and reaping continue, right?!

By the time the prophet Nathan confronts David, the jig is up, and all that's left is for him to acknowledge his wrongdoing. In Psalm 51, David reveals his true heart for God and regret for his poor judgment. In verse three, he says, "For I know my transgressions, and my sin is ever before me."

We know how this plays out: David repents, but he has to live with the consequences, the fruit if you will, of his sin. The child dies after Bathsheba gives birth, and a bunch more chapters in the Bible provide an account of the "harvest" that comes because of David's sin. He sowed to the flesh and reaped destruction.

That's not the end of David's story, however. For the rest of his life, he sowed good seed that demonstrated his understanding of God's sovereignty and his role as king of Israel.

As an interesting side note, God's grace is on full display with David throughout his life, especially as he grapples with the consequences of his sin. David clearly understands God's grace and is broken in the wake of his repentance.

What we learn from David is that we can allow the Holy Spirit to sow good things into us. We can also learn from our mistakes and resolve to draw near to God as we grow in Him. We can watch good programming. We can listen to good material. We can surround ourselves with good people. We can spend time with God. We can respond to the conviction of the Holy Spirit.

If we find ourselves shying away from things that we know "just aren't right," that's a good thing, too. We need to be sensitive to the Holy Spirit and invest in things that build us up spiritually and draw us closer to God, not those that drive us away. Then, we need to wade back into the world and sow good seed into people's lives.

My Binge-watching Battle

Quite a few years back, I was binge-watching a terrible post-apocalyptic program I couldn't get away from, *The Walking Dead*. I didn't just watch it. I was into it, like, "Yeah, I'd survive that. I'd keep my humanity and be one of the good guys." Who was I kidding? I know. I can't believe it myself now when I think about it. I have always had an interest in the end of humanity kind of stuff and "Could I survive?" stories. I'm not alone since it is a blockbuster program.

I was robbing myself of sleep, which, of course, was already a bad start, but I also found myself increasingly anxious, agitated, and irritable as I watched season-after-season. I was sowing to my flesh something I could not forget.

I was definitely grieving the Spirit and confided to Sara, my wife, that I wanted to be accountable to her. I didn't want to watch that garbage or anything like it ever again. I felt convicted and needed to confess it to someone and ask her to hold me to it. She did, gladly, since she couldn't understand why I would even want to watch such an awful program in the first place.

I'm telling you this to encourage you to take an audit of what you are sowing and may be reaping as a result. We have a saying in our house — most often when I'm being a clown jumping around in my bathing suit — "Well, we can't unsee that." It's like that with what we sow into our lives. God forgives us, but from a stewardship standpoint, we have still sowed something that drives us further from Him, not closer. We wasted His time and ours. That's equivalent to disobedience since He gives us time to use for His glory.

I hope you can see how, like David, I was feeding my flesh and rejecting God in so doing. For me, Galatians drives home the point that sowing and reaping is very much a part of stewardship and reinforces its holistic nature, encompassing every aspect of life.

Certainly, we can connect the dots easily with giving, that if we give, there will be a reward in return. We are used to the idea that effort produces results. It is wired into our psyche. And giving feels really good for most people, regardless of whether their motive is personal pride versus glorifying God.

Sowing, Reaping, and the Prosperity Gospel

As I grow in my Christian journey and understanding of God's Word, I find myself butting heads with "prosperity preaching."

From what I can discern, I don't think God cares either way about money; He only cares about our hearts toward it.

If money is an idol, God will chip away at you in that area and may even take it away to get your attention. He wants to be foremost in your life. The first of the Ten Commandments in Exodus 20 says, "You shall have no other gods before me." It is a recurring theme throughout the Bible. It has nothing to do with whether you deserve more or less money. It's about Him trying to break money's hold on you in a way that only He knows will work. He may give you more to test you, see if He can trust you with it, and shape you into the person He wants you to be. But, again, it's not about you; it's about you acknowledging Him.

It is important to say I have not seen a "tit for tat" measuring cup approach to sowing and reaping in my personal journey with money. I have found God has filled my life with blessings that I could not buy. He has given me more and more of the fruit of the Spirit. In some cases, He has also given me more money, and I could tell He wanted to work with me to use it for His kingdom. In some seasons of my life, He has taken money away because my heart was drifting to a fleshly longing for it.

I'm reminded of the story of Zacchaeus, the tax collector who climbed a tree to get a better look at Jesus. He said he would commit to paying off those he had stolen from and cheated. Meanwhile, the rich young ruler walked away heavy-hearted because he loved his position and possessions more.

False teachers who preach a prosperity "gospel" that justifies the church's insatiable appetite for this world is reason for alarm. God's only interest in money is how we use it, whether to build His kingdom or our own.

2 Peter 2 warns the church to be on guard. If the teachers and preachers you tune into are glorifying themselves and telling you to do the same by making it about you and not God… Run!

Like Joseph did from Potiphar's wife… Run!

Conclusion

God's Word directs us to be mindful of why, how, what, where, and when we sow. All we sow, all we do, where we spend our time, and who we spend it with; all we see, all we consume with our body, eyes, ears, and mind, will bear either good or bad fruit.

Galatians 6:7-10 warns us, "Do not be deceived, for the one who sows to his own flesh will from the flesh reap corruption. And let us not grow weary of doing good, for in due season we will reap, if we do not give up."

This has become more evident to Sara and me in recent years as we continue to step out in faith. We talk a great deal about the programs we watch and their influence on our girls and us. We talk about our finances and who, where, and how we should give, and if our time should back those financial gifts.

Luke 6:38 says, "Give, and it will be given to you. A good measure, pressed down, shaken together, and running over, will be poured into your lap. For with the measure you use, it will be measured to you."

Luke 16:19-31 tells the story of the rich man and Lazarus, a poor beggar. In the story, each receives his respective reward for what they sowed in life. Lazarus is in heaven; the rich man is dispatched to hell. It is interesting to note that once the rich man resigns himself to his fate, he wants Abraham to send Lazarus to warn his five brothers not to make his mistake.

My cry for the church that today embodies the nameless rich man is to repent before it's too late to turn away from the world and its terrible influences. Sow and reap that which is good and turn towards God.

THE TAKEAWAY

Bible stewardship cannot be divorced from an understanding of the sowing and reaping principle. The two are intertwined. What we sow and how much we sow will come back to us in the same measure. Like David, we can sow the wind and reap the whirlwind, or we can sow good seed that reaps an eternal harvest.

Describe a time when you sowed into your flesh something you knew wasn't good for you. (e.g., a relationship or lifestyle choice)

When was a time you sowed good things into your soul and spirit that made you feel closer to God?

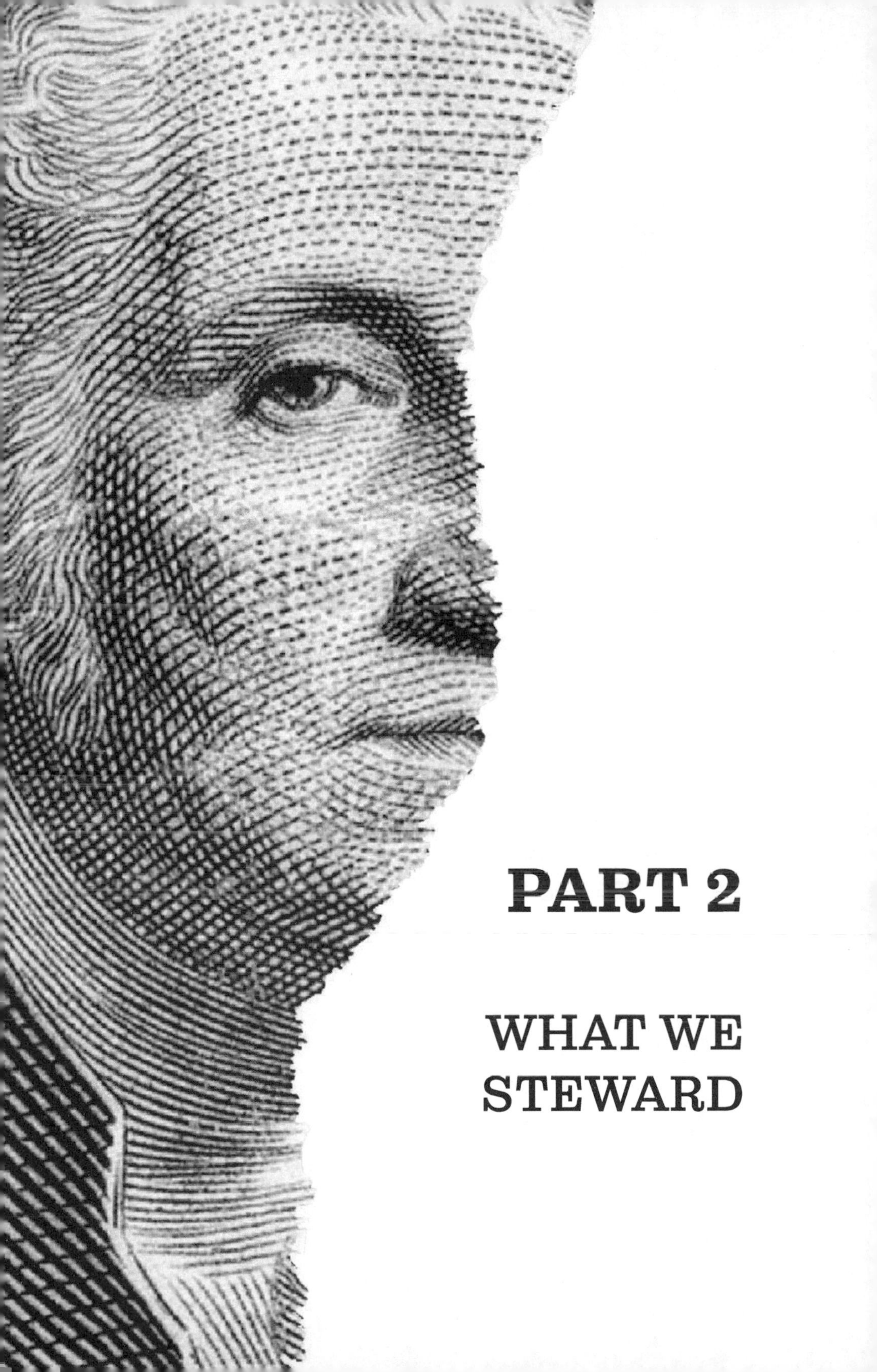

PART 2

WHAT WE STEWARD

CHAPTER 6

Time: 168 Hours a Week

"All men think it is only the other man who is mortal."
—Greek Philosopher

"Teach us to number our days that we may gain a heart of wisdom."—Psalm 90:12 (Attributed to Moses)

I watched my Father drown and suffered for many years to follow. I saw that event as a curse from God, hands down the worst thing that could ever occur to me — and for a season, it was. I have had to endure harder things since. Now, I look back and see what a gift losing my father was. I recognized that was his appointed time, and nothing I could have done to save him would change that.

It has given me a deep sense of my mortality that I see others lack. I watch other people act as if they have no expiry date. Men and women work like they will get to enjoy the fruits of their labors for all eternity. But as Ecclesiastes 5:15 says, naked we came and naked we shall return with nothing to show for our toils.

I work hard, but I am keenly aware that at forty-four years old, I am already past my dad's expiry date (he died at forty-three) and, at best, halfway through my life expectancy. As I think about the brevity of life, Psalm 90:12 comes to mind. It says, "Teach us to number our days that we may gain a heart of wisdom." So does Isaiah 40:6-8. It points out that our lives are like grass that withers and is gone.

Time is the first milepost on our stewardship journey. Why? Because unlike the many other resources God gives us, time is not something we can remanufacture, recreate, or get more of. It doesn't matter if we are one of the wealthiest people on the planet or the poorest; we each get twenty-four hours a day, one hundred sixty-eight hours a week. We sleep for forty or fifty of those, work forty or fifty, which leaves sixty to eighty for ourselves.

What the Lord is looking for is how we use those hours. How do we see our work? Is it something we just do for a paycheck, or are we working as unto the Lord? (Colossians 3:23) God wants us to trust Him to open doors and provide rather than act like a duck in the water — appearing calm on the surface but with legs paddling feverishly back and forth underneath. He knows we only have so much time. The question is, are we giving it to Him first? Are we saying, my time is yours, Lord, help me to use it wisely to further your kingdom?

He talks about that in Matthew 6:26-30: "Look at the birds of the air, for they neither sow nor reap nor gather into barns; yet your Heavenly Father feeds them. Are you not of more value than they? ... Consider the lilies of the field, how they grow: they neither toil nor spin; and yet I say to you that even Solomon in all his glory was not arrayed like one of these. Now, if God so clothes the grass of the field, which today is, and tomorrow is thrown into the oven, will He not much more clothe you, O you of little faith?"

God knows what you need, but if you refuse to steward His time by trusting Him, you will consume every minute scrambling and striving. On the other hand, if you trust Him, He will open up time for you to give it back, doing the things that matter most in His eyes.

Certainly, we need time to sleep and earn an income. It's how we use our free time that I'm mainly referring to. We waste a staggering amount watching TV, scrolling through social media, and pursuing things that pull us away from God and His Word.

A lack of stewardship also keeps us from reserving time to interact with and serve other people. Without time in your calendar, you can't engage with people, listen to them, or come alongside to help them with their struggles — you are too busy dealing with your own.

"THE TROUBLE WITH TIME IS YOU THINK YOU HAVE IT."

—BUDDHA

Time Stewardship and Personal Motivation

If you think about people striving, busy raising their profile, seeking acknowledgment from others, you have to ask, what's the motivation? Is it born out of pride, jealousy, or wanting to be the center of attention? Their insecurities are hijacking them to trade their time to make a name for themselves. Like moths to the flame, they are drawn to lesser things because they aren't clear where God is calling them to spend their time and energy. Perhaps they don't know God or care who He is. What concerns me are those of us who profess to know Him. Who are we trying to glorify with our time, Him or ourselves?

What's the antithesis? Being at peace, knowing who you are in Christ, with no need to prove anything to anyone. You are focused solely on what He wants you to do. However, the only way to get there is to spend time with God in His Word and prayer, asking for guidance.

How Do You Spend Your Time?

If the Lord asked you how He wants you to spend your time, how would you answer? You only have so much of it, so be mindful of how and where you use it. If what you're doing is not what God has called you to, don't do it. Even Jesus had limits on His time. As the God-man, He couldn't be everywhere at once. That's why He went to prepare a place for us and sent the Holy Spirit to dwell within us and be with us.

If Jesus took on limitations, He doesn't expect us to be everything to everyone. He does expect us to be obedient to what He has put in front of us for our time that day. That can be the most mundane, simple thing, but who knows the impact that temporal expenditure of time could have on eternity for us and others.

I can remember chatting with my friend Mark, the missionary in Peru, about limitations. There were so many kids living in difficult circumstances. The school, housing, and staff could only support so many. I said, "Mark, there are so many kids that need help. How do you not become completely overwhelmed by the need?" He responded calmly, "We are only responsible to God for the ones He puts in front of us." He explained that if more people listened, responded, and obeyed God, the need would be met.

His advice made me think of Jesus's word: "The harvest is plentiful, but the workers are few." Just think, there may be those in need in this world that have "your name written on them," waiting for God to send you. God is willing to do His part. Are you? As Isaiah said, "Here am I, Lord. Send me."

Let me illustrate with a personal story. While I was still in what I've often referred to as my wondering years where I questioned, wrestled with, and ran from God, He chased after me. He sent men who were strong and resolved in their faith to influence me and act as a father to the fatherless. (Psalm 68:5-6) He also sent some amazing friends into my life who were very deliberate and gracious about their faith. As Proverbs 18:24 says, "There is a friend who sticks closer than a brother." John McKay is one such person.

John was one of my best friends in high school. He was always the stronger believer. I was the prodigal, but John stayed faithful and fruitful. He continually offered his time and never gave up on me or our friendship, even when I strayed.

In 2010, when I was struggling with my marriage, he thought nothing of taking time to help me. John dropped everything to spend a few days encouraging me. He left his family, and flew from Vancouver, British Columbia, to Toronto, Ontario, where I was working. It was a fantastic blessing and so badly needed as I grappled with the dynamics of a crumbling marriage. It was a huge investment of his time and a sacrifice for his family as well.

God had allowed me to do the same for John some years before. John had moved to British Columbia after high school to attend bible college. Later, he went to college to become an educator and remained in the province to pursue a career as an elementary school teacher.

In his late twenties, he had a round of grand mal seizures. John had no family in British Columbia to support him and was living alone. He also lost his driver's license for a year due to the seizures. As a result, he was down and out, alone, facing some severe inadequacy issues, lower than low.

When I heard what happened, I booked a flight to BC the next day. John couldn't believe it when I showed up, but I told him that he had invested in me for so long, it was time for me to do the same for him. We hung out for a week, just like in high school. On one particular day, we went water skiing in the lake district outside Vancouver. (I was petrified he would have a seizure and drown but didn't tell him that.)

While driving back to the city later that day, John suddenly reached across the seat from the passenger side. (I was driving because he had lost his license.) He grabbed my arm and went into another full-blown grand mal seizure. In shock and unsure of what to do, I quickly pulled the car to the side of the road, put a pen in his mouth so he wouldn't bite his tongue, and rushed to a nearby hospital, where he was admitted to the ER.

I got to see firsthand what a grand mal seizure does to a person. John had complete memory loss. He didn't know where he was or who I was and could not remember the week's events or the time we spent together. It was jarring for both of us for different reasons.

The hospital staff inserted an IV into his arm and began assessing his situation. After a few hours, his memory slowly returned. He must have asked me at least a dozen times what happened. I would respond and then watch in anguish as, each time, he reacted despondently and with despair.

Now, nearly twenty years later, a guy who thought he had no future is a devoted husband and Father with a beautiful family and thriving career. He continues to be one of the greatest encouragers in my Christian walk, regardless of where I am in it or how far away from each other we are. Stewarding my time with John cemented a life-long friendship and our journey for Christ as brothers. That same friendship is a mutual source of encouragement in our respective walks with Jesus as we lead our families.

Stewarding Your Time to Honor God

I cannot overstress the importance of stewarding time in a way that honors God. Here are some action steps to help you begin.

Set a schedule and stick to it. Schedule devotional time with the Lord, downtime, exercise time, family time, and time to invest in others. That sounds like a lot, I know, but if you don't set a schedule, you won't do it. You have to be intentional, deliberate, and committed. Create a morning routine that gets your day started right. My wife's devotional time, where she writes in her journal, is at 6:15 a.m., followed by exercise. For me, it's a coffee in bed where I read and spend time in prayer. Exercise is an end-of-day thing.

Put "pink" in your calendar. I put pink in my calendar each week for daddy-daughter time. It is as non-negotiable as a client meeting. Whether it's time with your spouse, family, a close friend, or God, make the time you set aside irrevocable. Book it in advance. Don't fly by the seat of your pants.

Create accountability. That is easy for me as a business owner; I have accountability to employees and clients. Likely, that's not your situation, so find an accountability partner — your spouse, a close friend, a mentor — someone who will hold you responsible for your time stewardship commitment. My assistant at my office guards date night or daddy-daughter time with a vengeance for me.

Delegate and use the help of others. Regardless of who you are, I am willing to bet there are people you can rely on. Only Simon and Garfunkel were "rocks" and "islands." Don't go it alone.

Budget in margin. Many of us have a guilt complex if we schedule time to do nothing. It is the North American lie that busy people are important people. We are hardwired to believe that if we're not doing something, we're lazy.

Scheduling downtime doesn't mean you're doing nothing. Instead, you're taking time to recharge your battery, whether engaging in an activity you enjoy, spending time with friends, or simply relaxing. I love getting outdoors and hiking. Spending time in God's creation is good for my soul; it brings me to a place of prayerful meditation. There are no distractions. (I leave my cellphone at home.)

THE TAKEAWAY

When we fill our calendar to overflowing with busyness, we have no time to develop our relationship with God or invest in other people.

James 4:13-16 cautions us against being prideful about the use of our time and not seeking God's will in how we spend it. He reminds us that we are but "a vapor that appears for a little time and then vanishes away." Instead, we should say, "If the Lord wills, we shall live and do this or that."

In what ways do you spend your time?

How much time during the week do you waste? (Write down the number of hours you spend watching TV, on social media, etc. Add it up and subtract the total from the sixty or seventy hours you have free from work and resting.)

What needs to change to be a better steward of the time God has given you?

What action step can you commit to begin?

CHAPTER 7

Energy: Lord of All or Not at All?

> "Unless the Lord builds the house, they labor in vain who build it; unless the Lord guards the city, the watchmen keep awake in vain. It is vain for you to rise up early, to retire late, to eat the bread of painful labors; for He gives to His beloved even his sleep."—Psalm 127:1-2

The dictionary defines energy as the strength and vitality required for sustained physical or mental activity. I prefer to think of energy from a stewardship perspective as "enthusiasm." I discovered a long time ago that if I'm enthusiastic about something, I can go for extended periods after my physical energy is depleted.

(Note: While God wants us to be enthusiastic about His work, He also wants us to move at a pace He sets that we can handle long-term. He doesn't want us burned out, but balanced.)

The word enthusiasm is derived from the Greek *entheos*, which means God within (i.e., the Holy Spirit). Serving the Lord, engaging in kingdom-building work, and sharing the good news of the Gospel has a positive, energizing element to it. The energy born of enthusiasm is that fire in your belly, which says this is so fantastic you just want to keep going.

Enthusiasm comes from being gripped by something greater than ourselves. The theologian John Piper put it well when he said in a sermon, “People who make a difference in the world are not people who have mastered a lot of things. They are people who have been mastered by a very few things that are very, very great.”

You don’t need a high I.Q. or E.Q. (emotional intelligence quotient) for your life to count. It doesn’t require good looks, a good family, or a good school. You just have to know a few basic things, be gripped by them, and be willing to lay your life down for them. Anyone can make a difference in the world, because it isn’t you; it’s what you’re gripped with.

Striving vs. Thriving

> “If you look at your life as a place to find happiness, you will be disappointed and confused.”—C.S. Lewis

I have observed in my growth as a follower of Jesus that if I’m not engaged in God-honoring stewardship of my time, talent, and resources, investing in others and the kingdom, I’m likely sowing to my flesh. It takes examination of self and self motives. In that case, you’re likely driven by selfish pursuits, trying to find happiness in this life. There’s nothing permanently energizing about spending our time on ourselves. It may bring momentary pleasure but lacks transcendent value. That is why contentment always escapes our society.

Paul taught that contentment is something we teach ourselves as we fix our hearts on God. (Philippians 4:11-13) It is a state of mind that comes from surrendering our souls to God's providence and omniscience. It comes from not being in want or lusting after everything the world has to offer.

It is energizing to say, "I am content. I am where God wants me to be. I'm tuned into the Spirit, sensing God's call, taking the time to spend with Him, and experimenting with my talents to figure out what He wants me to do." Energy like that is born out of obedience, knowing you are in the center of His will. I like to call it "being in the spiritual zone."

> **"NO ONE ELSE IS SUPPOSED TO UNDERSTAND YOUR CALLING; IT WASN'T A CONFERENCE CALL."**
>
> **—UNKNOWN**

When you are in "the zone," don't let anyone knock you out. Even Jesus had to tell Peter to get behind Him — "Get behind me, Satan," is how Jesus put it — when Peter was trying to distract Him from His calling. (Matthew 16:23)

Assuming we know our *what* and *why* regarding our calling in life, then when do we rest? My answer: when you are tired. Think of those sins that nag at you, causing you to stumble in your walk with the Lord. When are they the strongest? When you are tired, worn out, and spiritually drained. Recognize that fact and protect yourself from succumbing by taking time to rest and reenergize.

Elijah was where God wanted him when he confronted the prophets of Baal. After his victory, his energy waned, and his spirit was overtaken by fear. (1 Kings19:5-8) Can you believe that? Elijah saw the entire army of God, defeated the prophets of Baal, and then was "overtaken by fear!" Why? Because he was drained of energy, physically depleted, and emotionally and mentally worn down.

We live in a society that prides itself on being busy. It is a status symbol, a badge of honor. For some, it's their house, their car, their money, or their family that keeps them occupied. For many, it's their schedule.

Pride in *self* is our idol. I was certainly guilty of it. People would say, "Hey Jon, how's it going?" to which I would respond, "I'm swamped" or "It's been hectic," or the trump card of all busy cards in the deck, "Man, I've been so busy, and business is goooood!" Can you say "ego!"

I didn't realize how the only person who cared was me until my doctor diagnosed me with burnout at age thirty-eight. I was running hard, from what I did not know, but I had to get a handle on it. It reminded me of that old country music song by Alabama about being in a hurry to get things done. This played in my head constantly.

That's when I realized I wasn't trusting God; I was trusting in myself and my abilities. I wasn't resting and waiting on Him as Isaiah 40:28-31 describes. In my arrogance, I thought that I could build my castle in the sand with the limited time and energy He allotted me. The worst part is, I was doing that while His castle lay in ruins — and it was costing me everything I held so dear. An old saying goes, "If he is not Lord of *ALL*, then he is not Lord at all." I will admit, I'm a slow learner but an eager one. How about you? What is consuming all your energy?

Rest Is God's Design for Us

I am a runner. I have loved running since I was a kid. I enjoyed track and field in school. When I joined the military, all they did was make us run. We would run every day, several times a day, sometimes in full combat gear with an eighty-pound rucksack. I loved it! It gave me time with my thoughts. When everyone else was winded, I was by default granted the floor to do all the talking, which I also loved!

Guys would fall out of formation "tossing their cookies," but I was like Forrest Gump. I never seemed to tire of running. I know now it's because I do a lot of thinking while I run… and I can do a lot of thinking! Today, we have smartwatches that can tell us everything short of what we had for breakfast. My watch tells me how many hours of REM sleep I got last night and the week's average. It counts the number of steps taken, and calories burned, monitors my heart rate, and even my stress levels to the minute. I love it, and I have had several over the years. It has tuned me in to how important and interconnected everything in my life is.

Sleep isn't as restful depending on what and when I consume

food and drink. If I don't exercise, I'm restless, and anxiety can creep in. If I don't rest, I can't get my work done, nor do I have the energy to exercise or do my work effectively. So I spiral up or spiral down depending on how I steward my energy.

We know that approximately thirty-three percent of our time is spent sleeping (if we are doing it correctly). The remaining sixty-six percent shouldn't be spent doing nothing but work.

What are we doing to give our body, soul, and spirit rest throughout the week? God's Word says rest is essential. In Genesis 2:1-3, after creation, God rested. In Exodus 20:8-11, He told Moses, via the third of ten commandments, "Hey gang, besides not stealing, lying, killing, and all that other important stuff, it would be a good idea if you all took one day out of seven to rest cause y'all need it. And I'd love to spend some of that time you are in short supply of with you since I took the time to, well, you know... make you." Even Jesus withdrew repeatedly from the crowds to, you guessed it, rest.

If God rested — which I think was more of a template for us than something He needed — and if Jesus, having taken on the frail body of a man, had to rest, then it stands to reason that humanity was not made for the fast-paced world we live in today. (The author John Eldredge points this out in his books *Wild at Heart* and *Get Your Life Back.*)

We are all running around most days on empty and can't get off the hamster wheel. Why? Because we don't want to. Because we don't really trust that God will provide. When Jesus says in Matthew, "Look at the birds of the air who neither sow nor reap." What do we think He means? He said it: "Don't worry." We need to stop striving if we want to start thriving.

Worry Steals our Energy

In Matthew 11:28, Jesus said, "Come to me, all who labor and are heavy laden, and I will give you rest. Take my yoke upon you, and learn from me, for I am gentle and lowly in heart, and you will find rest for your souls. For my yoke is easy, and my burden is light."

When I think about how little time we are afforded, it leads me to believe that God doesn't want us carrying the burdens of the world on our shoulders. He wants us to give those burdens to Him.

Worry has been the greatest robber of a restful spirit in my life. We worry about so many things, don't we? It's like carrying a sack of potatoes around on your back. Each potato represents one thing we worry about: things from our past, things in our future that often don't even materialize, and things we can't control, like global politics or a viral pandemic.

1 Peter 5:7 says, "Cast all your anxieties on Him because He cares for you." Given all the noise, why are we so resistant to resting in Him? Can I suggest it's often out of pride or a lack of understanding of God's magnitude? Job 38-42 is a powerful reminder of who God is. It took Job an entire book of the Bible to get it. Finally, he says, "I know You can do all things and that no purpose of Yours can be thwarted."

I have heard it said that when you start understanding the majesty of Christ, you stop asking why and start trusting the *who*. Job makes me feel better about the twenty years of my life I wasted dodging God… but only a little better. Still, it's nice to know there are other slow folks like me whom God didn't give up on. We think that our striving somehow will change the outcome of the game. Or that we are so important that we need to be at the center of what He is doing instead of acknowledging it's much more about Him than us.

Apart from working hard for Him (Colossians 3:23; 2 Thessalonians 3:6-15), we don't need to strive. Unfortunately, we are more like poor Martha (Luke 10:38-42), who was working away tirelessly, frustrated with her sister Mary, who chose to sit at Jesus's feet listening to Him teach. Seeing Martha's stress, Jesus said, "Martha, Martha, you are anxious and troubled about many things, but one thing is necessary. Mary has chosen the good portion, which will not be taken away from her." He would likely say the same to us.

So put down your smartphone, give Him your time, and He will restore your energy. To strive is to live life with a scarcity mindset. And to live with a scarcity mindset, I would respectfully suggest, borders on blasphemy. Don't fall into the fowler's snare of life. Don't be the seed that gets choked off on the path and doesn't take root out of fear and worry. Doing so means you don't believe God can or will provide.

You can trust Him with your family. He loves your children and your spouse more than you. You can trust Him with your finances and your business. You can trust Him with your trials. He will see you through to the other side. That's why, in Isaiah 26:3-4, he says, "You keep him in perfect peace whose mind is stayed on You because he trusts in You."

Energy Zappers

I learned that I have to guard my energy closely. Even though it's renewable, unlike our time, energy can be zapped quickly, so we need to be mindful of what drains us. We have to ask, is what we're doing building us up or tearing us down? That could be anything: relationships, business decisions, leisure activities, T.V., or social media… you name it.

For instance, how many of us have binge-watched a T.V. show for hours and then wished we hadn't? We're tired due to lack of sleep and feel guilty because the content wasn't that great to begin with. It was a waste of time and energy, right? The same is true when we operate out of the flesh, not the Spirit, when we're focused on selfish ambition and not surrendering to the Lord's direction.

Another story from my own life illustrates my point. Some years ago, I got it in my head that I wanted to spend a year sailing when I retired. "The kids would be off at university; I'm retiring at forty-nine and going sailing," I thought and said to my wife, "and you're coming with me!" No selfish idolatry disguised in there anywhere, eh?

It would still be several years until I retired, of course, so Sara and I decided to design and build our own catamaran while we worked toward filling our retirement barns. (Luke 12:19-21) We hired a marine architect to draw up blueprints for a fifty-two-footer. It was going to be a beautiful, custom boat with features you wouldn't find in a typical catamaran, including a king-sized bed on the main deck and some fantastic performance enhancements.

We found an old twenty-foot Hobie Cat to build a prototype, stripped it down, and completely rebuilt it. We ordered the best sails from Australia money could buy, had the architect design unique features like retractable daggerboards, and loaded it with carbon fiber. The boat is a fantastic piece of nautical handiwork.

It's red, looks like a streak on the ocean as it flies by without making a sound — and is entirely useless.

Allow me to explain.

There were problems from the start. For one, we hired a boat builder who turned out to be slower than molasses on a winter's day. Four years passed before it was ready, and the bills kept piling up to the tune of sixty-five thousand dollars.

You read that right. I spent sixty-five thousand greenbacks on a boat that I can sell for no more than fifteen thousand… and that's to a person in the Bahamas! Remember, we live in Nova Scotia, where the boating season is five months long, give or take.

The Bible says in Proverbs 26:11, "As a dog returns to its vomit, so a fool repeats his folly." I made a hefty financial investment and had no peace about it but would not give up on the project. To paraphrase, I was having a dog's breakfast with this boat.

I didn't listen to the Lord. I didn't even ask the Lord. Instead, I used His resources to build a state-of-the-art catamaran that's now sitting in a field next to my house. I often look at it to remind myself to pray before I leap and not waste time, resources, and energy on something that I didn't ask the Lord about and He did not ordain. In short, I used God's resources to build an extremely heavy paperweight. I learned my lesson. (And I have a fantastic Hobie Cat for sale, in case you're interested.)

PICTURES OF THE VERY EXPENSIVE PAPER WEIGHT

Qualities of an Energy Steward

One of the most significant indicators that a person is an energy steward is that they have the emotional and spiritual reserves to invest in others. That is why one of the fruits of the Spirit is self-control. Conversely, people low on energy, who are not enthusiastic about the things of God, have no time for others. They lack grace for difficult situations and difficult people. They expect people to come to them pre-sanctified or not come at all. Doesn't that sound like the church at times today? We lack patience for the messiness of broken lives and hurting people. We have no energy or time because we are too busy striving, grinding the gears of our own life.

Energy stewards also remain confident even when things don't go the way they plan. They are deliberate, not easily discouraged, and turn setbacks into stepping-stones, executing their God-given vision with a great sense of peace, calm, and purpose. They exhibit the fruit of the Spirit and are not quick to anger or judgement but, instead, are remarkably open-handed, forgiving, and approachable. They draw people to them. That's why sinners loved Jesus so much. They felt safe with Him. I want to be like that to the world. As a Christ-follower, I want people to feel safe with me. What about you?

Steps to Becoming an Energy Steward

We can find many examples from scripture that help us understand how to steward our energy. Here are a few to consider:

Guard Your Heart

Proverbs 4:23 says, "Above all else, guard your heart, for

everything you do flows from it."

That includes keeping a watch on your energy to determine if it's being drained or used for God's purposes.

Stay in Fellowship with God

Nothing depletes your energy more than unconfessed sin. In Psalm 51, after committing adultery with Bathsheba, David prayed, "Purge me with hyssop, and I shall be clean; Wash me, and I shall be whiter than snow. Make me hear joy and gladness, that the bones You have broken may rejoice. ... Restore to me the joy of your salvation and grant me a willing spirit to sustain me."

Only after confessing and asking for God's forgiveness did David have the energy to do the Lord's work as king.

In a similar vein, Acts 3:19 tells us to "Repent and turn to God so that our sins may be wiped out and that times of refreshing may come from the Lord."

Don't Be Lazy

The Apostle Paul instructed the church in Rome to "Never be lacking in zeal, but keep your spiritual fervor, serving the Lord." (Romans 12:11) To put it bluntly, don't be lazy about your relationship with God.

Wait on the Lord

A favorite passage of mine, Isaiah 40:31, says that waiting on the Lord brings renewed strength and energy: "But those who wait on the Lord shall renew their strength. They shall mount up on wings like eagles; they shall run and not grow weary; they shall walk and not faint."

Being a high achiever used to overextending myself, occasionally I have to hit the reset button and repent of self-dependency. I recall a time in late March 2018 when I faced a period of fatigue with work. Having spent all my energies in growing my investment firm, I needed to follow Isaiah's instructions to wait on the Lord.

I reached out to God, saying that I no longer wanted to continue running my company unless He was in it. I remember praying, "Lord, I surrender this business to you; I'm not going to strive anymore but wait on you and let you set the tone. If you aren't in it, then why am I doing it?"

Since then, Sara and I have experienced peace surrounding my business and a renewed zeal for it. He revealed to me both my calling and my place in the world. My company has now become a means to an end. I serve my employees and clients with a fresh outlook. I sow and reap in a "marketplace" ministry throughout my workday.

Many of the people who have joined the company have been a blessing, and we have blessed them with a thriving culture. Best of all, our business has flourished as a result.

I stopped striving and started going to God with everything. Nothing was too small, whether it was an investment opportunity, correcting an employee, or another business decision. I don't know how to share what God has done other than to say He just *took over* when I *gave it over*. And I have to hand it over daily.

Jesus' Example of Energy Stewardship

Jesus modeled the need for rest to reenergize. His disciples would often find Him in prayer and quiet meditation. Mark 1:35 says that "very early in the morning, while it was still dark, He departed and went out to a desolate place and there He prayed."

Jesus also took time off before making major decisions.

"One of those days, Jesus went out to a mountainside to pray and spent the night praying to God. When morning came, He called His disciples to Him and chose twelve of them, whom He also designated apostles." (Luke 6:12-13).

Even as Isaiah 50:4 says, "Jesus woke every morning and went to the Lord in prayer preparing for the day and challenges ahead."

He also took time to rest after a heavy period of ministry. For example, Christ dismissed the crowd after feeding the five thousand and went up on a mountain by Himself to pray. (Matthew 14:22-23)

If Jesus needed to renew His energy to do his Father's work, how much more do we?

THE TAKEAWAY

Being a good energy steward means that we take time to connect with God. Only then can we have the enthusiasm and wisdom to fulfill His calling in our lives.

What comes to mind when you think of the word "energy?"

What is one way you may be wasting energy that you could put to good use otherwise?

Of the passages listed above, which one speaks to you the most and why?

CHAPTER 8

Mind & Body

"The Catholic novelist believes that you destroy your freedom by sin; the modern reader believes, I think, that you gain it in that way. There is not much possibility of understanding between the two." Flannery O'Connor

At this point, I think you get the overarching premise of this book is that God owns everything. That includes our bodies and minds. Therefore, we are responsible for being good stewards of how He made us physically and intellectually. Romans 12:1-2 instructs us to offer our bodies as "living sacrifices" and renew our minds to know God's will. Both are required to be good body-mind stewards.

Mind Your Body

If we view our bodies as our own, we may go to two extremes: pay no heed to what we put into it and how we treat it, or the opposite, worship it. If, however, we understand the body is the temple of the Holy Spirit, then we will accept, cherish, and take care of it as good stewards.

The Apostle Paul put it this way:

> "Do you not know that your bodies are temples of the Holy Spirit, who is in you, whom you have received from God? You are not your own; you were bought at a price. Therefore, honor God with your bodies." —I Corinthians 6:19-20

Christians and Alcohol Consumption

Sara and I have struggled with alcohol consumption regarding its physical, mental, and spiritual effects. As new Christians, we didn't feel any particular moral conviction one way or another. Many of our Christian friends we knew partook. A good friend of mine having read my transcript even suggested that I tread softly on this issue given people's mixed feelings around alcohol within the church. At the risk of sounding preachy, I decided to press forward with sharing my take on alcohol. I encourage you to search God's word and obviously decide for yourself what He says about this substance. I will say this, as young Christians who lived in the world and consumed alcohol and have seen the ravages on our society first hand and up close, our minds are resolute.

Drinking alcohol is endemic in Canadian culture, and it was part of our heritage and family dynamics growing up. There was no reason we would think anything negative surrounding its consumption or impact. We believed that it got the better of some people, but all and all, it was harmless. That's what we were led to believe. The church didn't seem to frown on it, depending on the circles we ran in, that is.

So where did that leave us as a couple? We observed, many people in the church turn to alcohol as a coping mechanism, much like the world does. They self-medicate to curb anxiety and stress rather than going to the Lord with their problems. We knew that in the world, it's because they don't know the Lord, so can you blame them? Having worked with Teen Challenge for many years, I have seen what alcohol can do to someone. I've seen how addictive the substance can be and how it destroys lives, families, and communities.

My grandfather was an alcoholic, in my opinion. He was a World War II vet who went through a lot in Europe, serving as an infantryman in the Canadian Armed Forces. He came home damaged. He didn't know how to deal with PTSD, so alcohol became his way of self-medicating and managing his difficult memories. For that generation, there was little else they could use to cope.

Sara's family also has many culturally embedded norms and it is generally accepted that alcohol use is a way of life. It's ever-present in our society and an honored guest at every occasion, good or bad. Jesus even made more of it at a wedding when His mom asked Him to. That sure would make a fella popular, wouldn't it?

We use alcohol to relax, socialize, grieve, and celebrate. And yet, in its purest form, it is poison. Drinking pure alcohol can kill you. You can run your car on it. You have to dilute it and add flavor to make it consumable so that you won't die.

And yet, knowing that, our society keeps consuming more of it. Sara said to me a few years back, "Jonathan, this is like pouring gasoline into our bodies on Friday night and then getting up early on Saturday, having a healthy shake, and heading out for a run. It's stupid." It sure resonated with me when she said that. I had had an internal dialogue for years about what good it was, along the lines of, "Is this lending itself to a life that goes deeper with Christ or draws us away from Him?"

When we both decided to follow Jesus and grew more and more eager to mature in Him, many Christians told us there was nothing wrong with drinking. From a theological perspective, you can argue that drinking alcohol is not a sin unless done excessively. Paul warned the Ephesians not to be "drunk with wine." In Galatians, he included "drunkenness" as one of the works of the flesh along with sexual immorality and idolatry. Paul also told the Corinthian church that "everything is permissible for me," but added, "not everything is beneficial." In 1 Timothy 5:23, he said a little wine was good for digestion. Countless passages talk about the danger of a loose tongue and the lack of self-control excessive drinking can cause.

So, there we were. Some folks seemed fine with it; others never said much but simply shied away from us with no explanation. That was our "Christian" circle. In the end, we concluded both were wrong. Let me explain. Our internal dialogue centered on the following. There is nothing good that can come from alcohol. There are lots of bad things that can come from it. Even if it is ok, why sit so close to the fire? Even if we don't get burned ourselves, others might. And if others could get burned and we influence them in that our actions suggest it's ok, then we would/could be responsible for the influence we have and that would be poor stewardship of those relationships by way of our influence. We saw enough of how alcohol destroys lives in the world and saw nothing that pointed us to Christ associated with alcohol when we came out of the world. In fact, we had to kind of tilt our head at Christians who drank socially as new believers and question what they saw as their end game with this stuff? What were they trying to achieve so far as their witness to the world? How in their mind were they being different as we are called to be in a world that is lost?

What I can humbly submit is that if I am in a situation with a friend that I'm pouring into spiritually and that friend doesn't know Christ and wants to "hash" out their struggles over a beer, I'll join them as a one off. It makes no difference to me if I consume alcohol. It simply serves no purpose for me as a believer. To me, that is going into the world to chase after someone Jesus loves and I'm meeting them where they are. But beyond that, it really serves no use for a believer and follower of Christ. Sara and I decided in the church there were two camps. We concluded the first camp were generally more interested in Jesus on their terms and didn't seem like they wanted to go deeper in their relationship with Him. I know that is harsh. But we felt they were looking to justify why they could drink alcohol regularly rather than asking why they should and what harm comes from it. We didn't want it to be a stumbling block in our life or others lives we interacted with. We felt that first camp wanted us to stay shallow and cursory for their convictional comfort. Meanwhile, as I said earlier in the book, the other group wanted us to arrive on the church's doorstep "pre-sanctified" and polished up with all the right answers. In the end, we needed to be stewards of grace to both and still prepared to wade into the world if need be, much like Jesus. A world where we were more focused on the lost and ministering to them than the found who seemed caught up in how close or far they should stand from the fire. Ironically, after saying all of that, both groups shunned us. There we were. Alcohol-free with no one to tell.

So far as alcohol is concerned, I would simply ask, why bother at all? Drinking may not be a stumbling block for one believer, but it could be for another, and Paul strongly advised the church not to cause a weaker brother to stumble. (Romans 14:13-23) If you are truly honest with yourself, you can admit that it's not drawing you closer to Jesus. It is a bad use of His time, energy, and money. It leads to nothing good, and none of the Spirit's fruit is brought out in a person who embraces this stuff.

Alcohol, we decided, is an addictive substance that can and will hook anyone who drinks it often enough. It is unbiased in its assault on your life and will destroy you given the chance. It has no good byproducts — unless you consider a loose tongue, violence, depression, infidelity, bankruptcy, and regret good by-products.

As we went deeper, we asked questions like, does drinking alcohol glorify God? How does alcohol affect us physically regarding our energy level or capacity to rest? What does it do to us spiritually? Are we able to spend time with God with a clear head tuned into the Spirit? Is even one morning lost to spending time with God good stewardship if we had one too many the night before? Try as we might, we could not point to one good thing about it.

Sara and I decided that the final "nail in the alcohol coffin" ("barrel" might be a more appropriate term) was that we simply weren't who we wanted to be under its influence. We weren't living out our values when we drank even one glass of wine privately or otherwise.

Taking all those factors into consideration, we decided not to consume alcohol any longer. It wasn't because we felt convicted drinking was wrong biblically. However, if we are honest with ourselves and God, that was part of it. (Now, it is a huge reason why we won't go back.) At the time, we just wanted to be more energetic, not be hungover or sluggish, and get up in the morning to spend time with the Lord in a more clear-headed manner. We also did not want to expose our kids to alcohol by keeping it in our home, continuing the cycle that our society tells us is perfectly fine. Also, I was tuned into our annual financial expenditure on alcohol and had to ask, "Is this what God would have me do as a steward of His wealth?" Again, being honest with myself and God, the answer was NO.

Getting rid of alcohol was big, really big. It was a step that, once taken, revealed more we could take towards knowing God better and trusting Him more. It broke chains we didn't even know existed, like diminished cognitive abilities and lethargy. The impact of alcohol on our body and mind should have been evident, but it wasn't.

With the firing of alcohol as our way to relax, celebrate, and, in short, self-medicate, we became conscious of what else we were doing to manage our anxieties and other negative emotions. We noticed that eating, shopping, travel, and more were often born from a lack of contentment or understanding of who we were in Christ.

The Problem of Over-consumption, Including Donuts!

My personal example and struggle around drinking too much alcohol isn't the only problem affecting our bodies. Consuming too much of anything isn't good, whether drinking, binge-watching TV, eating junk food, or too much food. Even sugar can be addictive. In an experiment, researchers took two rats and addicted one to sugar and the other to cocaine. They found that there were similarities between eating sugar and the drug effects of cocaine. They also found it was four times harder for the sugar-addicted rat to break the substance's dependence than the cocaine-addicted rat.

Sara and I are exceptionally good at emotional eating. Give us an apple pie and two forks on a bad day and that baby will be gone in no time. I eat emotionally when I'm fatigued, and my body is craving energy. Instead of eating the right things, however, I opt for sugary foods like chocolate, cookies and my fav of all, the peanut butter jar!

On the other hand, Sara is a major fan of donuts. One night, I suggested takeout from one of our favorite spots, that happen to make the best donuts from scratch. I added two to our order, or so I thought. Little did I know, Sara called the restaurant while I was heading to pick up the food, and added four more. When I got home she said, "Well, half a dozen sounded better than just two!?" She partook in almost all of them. The next day I found half a donut left. I was about to throw it in the garbage when she stopped me laughing and shouting, " No no! I'm going to eat that silly!"

Body Image Shame

Women are constantly bombarded with the insane idea of body image. Our daughters are assailed with the notion of what a "good body" looks like. Elementary school-aged girls are "smoke screened" into thinking they are undesirable if they aren't thin and pretty. Our society focuses only on the outside and spends no time on things that are lasting, timeless, and founded in truth.

This attitude is nothing new. It has always been with us. But Christians are called to look past what is skin deep. Like our Savior, we are to look at a person's soul and love them unconditionally, regardless of their body type. Failing that, our young women fall prey to eating disorders, their waist size, or, as I discovered in a recent discussion with my daughters, their "thigh gap."

If we celebrated values, such as truth, integrity, compassion, kindness, work ethos, loyalty, and more profound spiritual things, like grace and forgiveness, how many of our young women (and men) would be more resolved to not fall prey to the vain affections of their teenage suiters. How many strong and courageous women would be emerging into adulthood with a clear sense of self.

The same principle applies to the tongue.

James says that even though the tongue is a small part of the body, it has great power. It "corrupts the whole body" and "sets the whole course of one's life on fire." (James 3:6) James also says you can use your tongue to both praise and curse, comparing it to freshwater and saltwater flowing from the same spring. (James 3:11)

By that, James meant you can use your tongue to edify, build up, and encourage others or tear down, destroy, and malign. A good friend of mine said to me recently, "J, you can gossip with your tongue; it can either be negative or positive. If you are going to gossip, choose to gossip positively or not at all." An adage I have grown to love in recent years says, "A lie will go around the world while truth is pulling its boots on." Try to steer the rudder to say something positive about another person rather than spread rumors or a false report.

Your Mind... and Soul... and Spirit

Similarly, I have really noticed if what you eat and drink affects you physically, what you hear and see affects you mentally, emotionally, and spiritually.

The eyes and ears are gateways to your mind, soul, and spirit. Remember what we talked about under the characteristics of stewardship and sowing and reaping. Watching episodes of *The Chosen*, a television series about the life of Jesus, edifies you, but binging several seasons of shows like *Ozark* or *The Sopranos* diminishes you.

Matthew 6:22-23 says, "The eye is the lamp of the body. So, if your eye is healthy, your whole body will be full of light, but if your eye is bad, your whole body will be full of darkness. If then the light in you is darkness, how great is the darkness!"

Pornography's Devastating Effects

There is no greater darkness attacking men in particular today than pornography. It tears you down, weakening you morally and destroying you spiritually. Its darkness invades right through your eyes and goes straight to your heart. It is a secret sin that is not so secret to God and, yet for many church-going men, is hard to confess or find support.

The world today is tossing the lust of a woman's flesh at men everywhere. It is no secret that men and women are constantly assaulted with desire for the opposite sex through television, the internet, social media, magazines, billboards, and other forms of advertising.

If the worst happens, it goes on in secret until it comes to light, often in shame, having destroyed your soul and, quite possibly, your marriage and relationships. Lust of the eyes is the secret sin that does not stay a secret. From a stewardship perspective, it is a betrayal of what God has entrusted you with whether you are married or single. Instead of seeing the opposite sex or even same sex as a person to be cherished as a person, pornography teaches our young people to see the opposite sex as a commodity to be exploited and used with no thought of consequences to all the parties involved.

I'm not saying this to make any guy or gal out there feel ashamed. I'm saying it to elevate the sense of alarm. If this is you, find someone you can confide in and get counsel and help. Otherwise, you will stay in bondage until you do, and there is no good outcome.

Your Mental Acumen

We all have mental acumen that lends itself to a variety of abilities. When I look at people whose intellectual skills are different from mine, I am always amazed at where I'm weak and someone else is naturally strong.

Take a person who can sing, play, write, or produce music, for example. Musically, I'm like a squawking seagull, whether I try to play an instrument or sing. However, if you told me to unpack a problem, one where there's a challenging business scenario or adversarial relationship, or maybe a complexity leading to a potential win-win, and find a solution that creates buy-in, no problem. I have an innate ability to get people moving together collaboratively. I'm a problem-solver through and through.

Regardless of our skill sets, as stewards, we are to use these God-given mental aptitudes to produce results for the kingdom. But what if we can create music and are not doing it? Or lead people and don't? Or solve complex business problems and make money, but don't do it? Are we good stewards? The answer is, obviously, no. Instead, we need to ask the Lord what He wants us to do with our abilities to honor Him and bear kingdom fruit. It is squandering the gifts He entrusted you with not to shine where He made you to shine.

Being good stewards of our minds also means changing the way we think.

Paul said in Romans 12:2, "Do not conform to the pattern of this world but be transformed by the renewing of your mind." In Philippians 4:8, he said, "Finally, brothers and sisters, whatever is true, whatever is noble, whatever is right, whatever is pure, whatever is lovely, whatever is admirable; if anything is excellent or praiseworthy, think about such things." In 2 Corinthians 10:5, he commanded us to "take every thought captive to make it obedient to Christ." Nothing halfway about it, is there?

There are other verses about what our mindset ought to be as Christians, but the bottom line is this: Get rid of "stinkin' thinkin" and focus your thoughts on what honors God. Michael Hyatt is often heard saying, "Limiting beliefs are the barnacles on the hull of your ship and only slow you down… and once a year, you need to scrape them off."

Conclusion

Like the other stewardship building blocks listed in these chapters, the way you treat your body and mind reflects where you are and want to be spiritually. It is a decision you have to wrestle with, but so is this entire book when it comes to biblical stewardship.

I was challenged and I challenge you to ask, is what you are eating, drinking, watching, listening to, or thinking about drawing you closer to God or driving Him away? That is the lingering question. Finding the answer requires you to bathe it in prayer and the study of His Word and to engage with other Christians for accountability and leadership. Then, be a doer and not just a hearer. (James 1:22-25)

Body-Mind Stewardship Steps

Follow these steps to become a better steward of your body and mind.

Take Inventory

Take an inventory of what you're doing during a typical day regarding scheduled activities, look at it from the context of your body and mind, and then ask yourself, "Is what I'm eating, drinking, watching, or listening to good or bad?"

Start with the Desired Outcome

You have to be deliberate about what goes into your body, so start with the desired outcome. I want to be healthy and take care of the body God gave me, the temple of the Holy Spirit. Does what I'm doing help or hinder achieving that goal? Of course, you have to start where you are. It's similar to giving. If you're not giving anything, you can't jump to a ten percent tithe immediately. Neither can you go from zero to sixty to improve your health. Take small steps, but start. Plan your meals and time for exercise.

Take Your Thoughts Captive

Your eyes and ears are the gateways to your soul, so pay attention to what you watch, read, etc. It's essential to set the tone and captivate your thoughts. You can rehearse negative thoughts, or you can choose to entertain positive thoughts.

Draw a Line

A simple, practical exercise is to take a piece of paper, draw a line down the center, and list the pros on one side and cons on the other. The pros and cons are based on the question, does this draw me closer to Jesus or drive me further away? It's simple but decisive. I make it my goal to move toward the pros and away from the cons. If you have a sugar fetish, try cutting that out. If it's alcohol, drink less. If you're watching unedifying television programs, change the channel. If you aren't using your mental acumen for Him, start.

THE TAKEAWAY

Your body and mind are gateways to your soul and spirit. To be good stewards, make careful, God-honoring choices about what you allow in.

Are your body-mind habits drawing you closer to God or pushing Him away?

What is an area of your thinking that you struggle with? Why?

What is one step you can take to change your physical, mental or spiritual health?

What is something you can schedule as a good use of your time to steward your mind and body positively?

CHAPTER 9

Talents

Once you have given God your time, let Him restore your energy and renew your body and mind, you can begin to identify your talents and bring them to bear in ministry, be it in the workplace, your local church, or somewhere else in the world.

Talents come in two forms: those innate abilities you were born with and spiritual gifts (supernatural abilities) God gave you when you were born again. Will you use both to either build His kingdom or your own?

God has given all of us talents. Some people have more, others less. For example, my wife has a keen sense of discernment while I have the heart of an evangelist and can inspire and rally people using my leadership skills.

When you get clear on your talents, you must then acknowledge they are not yours to do with as you will, but as God wills. Using them for His glory is the key to stewardship.

The Relationship Between Spiritual Gifts and Innate Talents

Several passages in the Bible talk about spiritual gifts. Romans 12 lists them as prophecy, serving, teaching, encouraging, giving, administration, and mercy. I Corinthians 12 includes the word of wisdom, word of knowledge, gifts of healing, tongues, and interpretation of tongues.

Ephesians refers to the gifts as offices: apostle, prophet, evangelist, and pastor-teacher. I Peter mentions speaking and rendering service. James chapter 3 adds wisdom, a spiritual gift characterized by a person who is peace-loving, considerate, submissive, full of mercy and good fruit, impartial, and sincere.

Spiritual gifts expand on and supercharge innate talents — the two work in concert. For instance, someone who is intellectual and tuned into the Holy Spirit may begin to display spiritual wisdom and all the qualities that come with it.

Regardless of your particular gift-talent mix, God plugs you into His body and the world at large so you can develop all the assets you have to produce kingdom fruit.

Talent Stewardship Motivation: Who Gets the Glory?

How we use our talents always comes back to the *why*.

Paul says in Colossians 3:23 that whatever we do, we are to work at it with all our hearts, as working for the Lord and not for man. In our house, I refer to that as "Colossianing" — showing up with a willing, cheerful heart, going to work for an audience of one.

What's the connection between talents and our hearts? The answer is simple: Show me where you're spending your time and talent, and I'll show you where your heart is. For example, I'm really good with numbers and problem-solving skills. I can look at a business problem and see the "win-win" scenario clearly. I always ask, "Am I using that talent for myself and my glory or God's?"

If you are an athlete, it's the same: His glory or yours? If you are a talented musician: His or yours? Or in politics: His justice and mandate or yours? When it comes to the use of talents, the question incumbent on every Christian is always, am I building my kingdom while His house lies in ruins?

Paul frames the Colossians passage in the context of Christians as bondservants — God owns us and our talents. In using our abilities, we are to act as a servant for the master. Yet, I wonder how many Christians think about their motivations in the stewardship of their talents, whether they are based on pride, ego, jealousy, or to glorify God. The bridegroom at a wedding shouldn't be winking at the bride as she comes down the aisle, drawing attention to himself. That's what we do when we glorify ourselves ahead of God.

Daniel and Joseph: Heroic Talent Stewards

I love the book of Daniel. He "showed up." He and his friends had skin in the game.

Daniel 1:17 says, "As for these four youths, God gave them learning and skill in all literature and wisdom, and Daniel had understanding in all visions and dreams." Verses nineteen and twenty say, "And the king spoke with them, and among all of them none was found like Daniel, Hananiah, Mishael, and Azariah. Therefore, they stood before the king. And in every matter of wisdom and understanding about which the king inquired of them, he found them ten times better than all the magicians and enchanters that were in all his kingdom."

As we discuss stewardship, Daniel points to God, who gave him the wisdom and took no glory for himself. In chapter 2:27-28, "Daniel answered the king and said, 'No wise men, enchanters, magicians, or astrologers can show to the king the mystery that the king has asked, but there is a God in heaven who reveals mysteries and has made known to King Nebuchadnezzar what will be in the latter days.'" He goes on to interpret the king's dreams. (It's also worth noting that Daniel gets a promotion in line with the principle of sowing and reaping.)

Joseph is another hero whose story I have grown to love. It goes a little farther back — the story starts in Genesis 37 — but is just as impactful in demonstrating talent stewardship.

Joseph is the runt of the litter, the youngest of the bunch, and out of the gate, is spoiled by his father, Jacob. His brothers are jealous because Jacob loves him more than them. He had a head full of steam and many talents; yet, at age seventeen, he was not ready for what God had in store. It would take some refining. He had to be brought low to use them for God's glory.

Poisoned by hatred, Joseph's brothers conspire to kill him, but at the urging of one brother, Reuben, they opt to sell him to a caravan heading to Egypt. After he arrives, Joseph serves as a slave to Potiphar, a prominent Egyptian military officer. It isn't long before he rises to run Potiphar's entire household.

Joseph ends up being falsely accused of sexual assault by Potiphar's wife, the exact opposite of what actually transpired. She is the one who approached him. He displays tremendous character and self-restraint, running from her. In Genesis 39:9, Joseph shows his true heart by telling Potiphar's wife he will not sin against God. Much like his brothers' jealousy, the pride of a woman rejected leads to false accusations. Despite his loyalty to Potiphar and God, Joseph is tossed in prison. One could say this flies in the face of what we talked about regarding sowing and reaping. But does it?

Genesis 39:21-23 says, "But the Lord was with Joseph and showed him mercy, and He gave him favor in the sight of the keeper of the prison. And the keeper of the prison committed to Joseph's hand all the prisoners who were in the prison; whatever they did there, it was his doing. The keeper of the prison did not look into anything that was under Joseph's authority, because the Lord was with him; and whatever he did, the Lord made it prosper."

Joseph gets a job and does it well, clearly demonstrating, for the second time, a talent for administration and strength of character to persevere and trust God. The next talent Joseph brings to bear is in chapter forty, where he interprets two of the prisoners' dreams.

Much like Daniel, he points people to God, saying in verse eight, "Do not interpretations belong to God?" He asks the men to share their dreams so he can explain them. The story continues, and in chapter forty-one, Joseph is brought before Pharaoh to interpret his dreams. No pressure there, right?

If Joseph wasn't in it for the right reasons by this point, he would have been in trouble. But our "Karate Kid" of Genesis is up to the task because God had prepared him. His character, talents, and understanding of who God is are entirely on display.

In verse sixteen, Joseph says to Pharaoh, "It is not in me; God will give Pharaoh a favorable answer." Interpret the dreams he did, but he doesn't stop there. He also tells Pharaoh what to do for the pending famine God had revealed as part of his interpretation.

God grants Joseph ongoing wisdom in what actions to take to protect Egypt from the ravages of the famine. Pharaoh says, "Can we find a man like this, in whom is the Spirit of God?" He then adds, "Since God has shown you all this, there is none so discerning and wise as you are. You shall be over my house, and all my people shall order themselves as you command. Only as regards the throne will I be greater than you." Pharaoh concludes, "See, I have set you over all the land of Egypt."

Pharaoh makes Joseph his chief deputy, second in command of all of Egypt. Talk about sowing and reaping by way of being a good steward of God's gifts and talents.

I think if I were Joseph at that very moment, I would be looking around for the cameras. I'd be like, what just happened? All jokes aside, Joseph was obedient, didn't waiver, and brought his talents to bear wherever God put him. From a job in prison to the second most important role in Egypt, Joseph showed up and didn't give up. As we know, this was how God fulfilled His covenant with Abraham. Thanks to Joseph, God spared a remnant of his people from the famine's ravages, starting with his brothers, the ones who betrayed him.

So how do we show up like Daniel and Joseph? As talent stewardship and determination to glorify God increases, so does our fruitfulness, in two respects. First, we actively participate in the body and become fruit *producers*. Second, we also become fruit *bearers* as we see the fruit of the Spirit born out in our character — much like the fig trees in Jerusalem or the apple trees in our yard.

When you sell out and put your talents to work for Him *Colossianing*, the Spirit's fruit becomes the default in the way you conduct your life. Like Daniel and Joseph, God will use us if we are willing to go, without question, and give Him the glory.

The Family Journal, Turkey Drives, and Sleeping in the Cold

I'm no Daniel or Joseph, but I mentioned that leadership is one of my talents. I have to be intentional in its use. Sara would tell you that in our home, no matter how tired I am, I do not miss a single night leading our family in a devotional and prayer, recording events in the family journal. In my business, I rely on that talent to coax and encourage my employees to use their God-given abilities in marketplace ministry.

I also learned I have as much capacity to discourage and divide people as I do to encourage and ignite them. It comes back to my heart; am I in it for Him or myself? Am I "Colossianing" or being selfish?

Much like sowing and reaping, it would seem that for every talent God gives us, there is an equal and opposite fleshly counter-talent. For example, Joseph could have become arrogant and prideful as he rose to power in Egypt. He started that way when he shared his dreams of ruling over his brothers, father, and mother at age seventeen. But by the time God finished refining his character at age thirty, he was ready for what God prepared him to do. It's worth noting that he was a slave for thirteen years before entering Pharoah's service. During that time, Joseph never wavered from his duties or turned away from faith in God. He stayed in the game. Similarly, Daniel and his friends never waivered, even though their homes were sacked, they were hauled off in bondage, castrated, renamed and forced to serve in a foreign land surrounded by an ungodly culture. This speaks volumes, so far as how far we as Christians need to be prepared to go for Jesus. It separates those who are serious from those who aren't when, like Joseph and Daniel, we are really stripped of dignity and freedom. They had to ask… "Do I trust God in all His sovereignty?" Daniel never would have survived the lion's den had he not long before gotten clarity on who he served.

Lions' dens aside, like you, I'm still cutting my teeth on a lot of the basics. For me, those basics include two other significant ways that God has allowed me to use my leadership skills. One is an annual turkey drive we carry out during the holidays. The other is a community "sleepout" that we do on the coldest night of the year when temperatures can drop ten to fifteen degrees Fahrenheit below freezing (minus ten to minus twenty-five Celsius).

The Turkey Drive

I started an annual turkey drive in 2010 that now spans eight communities in our province. In one week, over a hundred donors and volunteers, along with several hundred business owners, feed more than five thousand people. We put bags of groceries together containing all the supplies a family of five would need for Christmas dinner. We also insert a copy of the Gospel of John, a schedule of community church services, and contact information for each church.

This year alone, we raised almost twenty-five thousand dollars to pay for everything, and it continues to grow. None of that would have happened without me, and the others involved, using our talents. It's hard work, and every year leading up to

Christmas, I ask myself, "Why am I doing this?" Then I talk to the people we are helping and see its impact on the volunteers and the communities we engage with. I know I am sowing into people's lives hope and love and most importantly the gospel of Jesus using my talents in a small way.

PICTURES FROM THE TURKEY DRIVE

The Sleepout

This example may bear some explanation for those of you not living in Canada. Each February, Canadians across the country designate one night as the "Coldest Night of the Year" and use it to benefit charities. Typically, people raise money, and communities hold a 5K run or walk.

Five years ago, I started thinking about another way to celebrate the event or, more accurately, take it up a notch. Instead of a 5K, I thought we would host a sleepout night where we set up tents in a park in Halifax, Nova Scotia, and use it as an opportunity to raise funds for Teen Challenge and to share the Gospel.

At the time, I spoke with the Teen Challenge leaders, saying, "We're Canadians; we know how to do snow and the cold." Reluctantly, they bought in. After making sufficient preparations that included getting permission from the city to use the park — you should have seen the look on their faces when we told them what we were doing — we went for it.

We rallied the community, got a guest speaker, secured propane heaters and food, held a Zumba class and treasure hunts, and did street ministry. Members of Teen Challenge shared their testimony about how God helped them get free of addictions. And homeless people showed up because they heard we had hot food donated by a friend who has a fifties-style diner. Businesspeople gave money to sponsor the event and, in some cases, did not have to sleep out themselves. Anyone who made it through the night (i.e., didn't chicken out and go home to their warm bed) got a free breakfast on me! The first year we had some forty people for breakfast across the street at the local diner. It was the best-tasting coffee ever!

I remember the first few sleepouts. Spenser Mason, the Teen Challenge development officer for the local center and former TC graduate, was overwhelmed, but we got through it. We just completed our fifth consecutive year despite Covid-19. (The organizers at the local center did a virtual sleepout, rallying people in four provinces to participate, so it was even better!) Next year, other cities across the country plan to take part in the same cause.

I share those stories not to draw attention to myself, but to illustrate the impact using your talents can have — first in the home, then the community, and potentially, the entire nation. Think about what the outcome of Joseph's story might have been had he given up in prison. God can use you and wants you to be a part of His plan for our lost world. He can do it without you, but He would rather not.

PICTURES FROM THE SLEEPOUT

JONATHAN WITH
MANLEY FEINBURG

Steps to Becoming a Talent Steward

As an entrepreneur, I think in terms of processes and systems, investment and measurable results, risk and reward. God in His sovereignty has exposed me to life as an entrepreneur as He has developed me for His purposes. As such, I naturally think the same way when it comes to stewarding our talents — risk, reward and results.

I think as believers, like so many heroes in the Bible and generations past, God expects us to take risks and step out for Him with what He has given us to work. It allows Him to create circumstances where He can reveal Himself when we can't see the way forward. God demonstrates how awesome He is in orchestrating every aspect of life on this spinning globe, down to the tiniest detail. So, what are some steps we can take towards stretching ourselves with the talents He has entrusted us?

First, take an inventory of your talents, both natural and spiritual. Take a personality test. Meyers-Briggs or the DISC Assessment are both excellent. Accompany that with a spiritual gifts inventory. Perhaps your church or denomination has one. The point is to get in tune with your talent mix. My family and I did a values assessment, compared where our values align and how we can encourage and hold each other accountable as we grow in our faith and understanding of God.

Ask God for direction. Once you have a handle on your talents, pray and ask God to direct you to where He wants you to plug-and-play. Ask Him to reveal the relationships, the right people, and the right places to use your talents.

Test the limits of your talents. Step out in their use. Just like an unflexed muscle never develops, your talents will never grow until you put them into service. Like 1 Peter 4:10 says, "Each of you should use whatever gift you have received to serve others, as faithful stewards of God's grace in its various forms."

Get out of your comfort zone. It will feel uncomfortable at first, but you will gain confidence the more you use your talents. I know I can run a marathon — I've done it many times — but can I do an Ironman competition? I won't know until I prepare and then try. Thankfully I'm not feeling called to. But if I were...

The first time I served on a board was like that. I knew I had well-honed leadership, business development, and problem-solving skills, but I was out of my element. As an entrepreneur, I was used to solving problems myself, not in a group setting. Now I serve on numerous boards for companies and non-profit organizations across Canada. My leadership skills have matured by working with others instead of on my own. I can see how God is using these boards to develop my character and self-restraint.

Seek wisdom and counsel. Ask God to give you a way to use your talents and seek counsel from others who have done it. The first part of James 1 and the latter part of James 3 walks us through how to seek His wisdom and heavenly council.

Read God's Word with frequency. As I worked on this book, I had to do a lot of reading and research into what God's Word said about stewardship. The deeper I dug, the better my understanding. Also, the frequency of time spent in the Word was powerful because I found myself meditating daily on what He was teaching me that applied to real-life interactions at work, in my home, and in social situations. Joshua 1:8 says, "Keep this Book of the Law always on your lips; meditate on it day and night, so that you may be careful to do everything written in it. Then you will be prosperous and successful."

Work with a coach. A coach can come in any number of forms — a pastor, mentor, or person with more life experience — someone who can help you recognize your talents and gifts. I have worked with coaches and mentors for over ten years, and they always point out, lovingly, my blind spots, pushing back when I don't. Like the writer of Hebrews instructs in chapter ten, verses twenty-four and twenty-five, "They 'admonish' me, 'spurring' me towards 'love and good deeds.' "

Learn by doing. When you step out, you will learn as much about what not to do as what to do. Your heart may be in the right place and your motivations pure, but if it's not your talent, it's not your talent, and that's okay. Soar with your strengths. Don't try to be all things to all people. You don't have to look hard to figure out your calling. Trust me; it's in front of you. But be a doer of the Word and not just a hearer. We have way too many hearers cluttering up the pews of the church today. He wouldn't have said His Word is a lamp unto our feet unless we needed light for walking, right?

Determine your motivations. Ultimately, the question comes down to who are you giving glory to? You or God. If you are promoting yourself, you are diluted to think your work is for Him. I've said it several times in this book; you are simply building your kingdom with His banner over the door. Don't let your vanity and pride get in the way.

Work with a team. Paul said that individually we are part of the body of Christ, not the entire body. The foot can't do the work of the hand or the mouth, or the work of the ears. Match your talents with those of others in the church and work as a team. This also helps create accountability, something that's especially important when it comes to that old self that wars for attention inside of us. We don't have to look very hard in the church today to see how great men and women of God have stumbled and fallen due to a lack of accountability and transparency.

Stay in tune with the Holy Spirit. Once you evaluate and begin to use your talents, don't move ahead of God. Get a sense of where He has put you in history — the time and for what purpose. The great pastor and theologian Dietrich Bonhoeffer knew his place in history — that God put him in Germany during the Nazi occupation to stand against tyranny — even though it would cost him his life. He was in the U.S. when the war broke out and knew God called him to go back and take on evil in his native land.

Evaluate the results and get feedback from others. As you begin to use your talents, assess what went well, what went wrong, and how to do better next time. Build systems and processes around yourself for success, ask others for feedback, and listen to the Holy Spirit.

Set new goals. Ask God what He would have you do next, and then go for it. Be prepared for some mundane sanding of the floor like Mr. Miyagi instructed his protégé Daniel to do. He may lead you to take on some audacious task, not unlike William Wilberforce, the British politician and philanthropist, who at the age of twenty-four, led a movement to bring down human slavery.

Invest in improving your talents. Don't just settle for good when you can strive for excellence. If you have academic acumen, then go with that. If it's managing financial resources, invest in that. If you are athletic, then work on improving in that area. You get the picture.

Investing in your talents includes an element of risk. You may fail, but you will never know unless you try. That's what the Parable of the Talents is all about. (Matthew 25:14-30) God is looking for risk-takers. The master rewarded those who invested what he gave them and rejected the one who hid his talent. He didn't just reject him; he stripped him of the talent and gave it to another. Not only that, but he also "cast the worthless servant into outer darkness. In that place there will be weeping and gnashing of teeth." That sounds like hell to me. So, personally, I'd like to be multiplying what I have been entrusted with rather than hiding it.

Let's frame this parable in a modern-day setting. A small business owner goes to his or her employee and says, "I paid you fifty thousand dollars last year. What have you done with my investment?" If the answer involves sitting passively in a cubicle collecting a paycheck, you can imagine the business owner will be disappointed and frustrated. What the master in the parable said, "You wicked servant," the business owner may translate to "You're fired." Remember, it's not our talents we are handling; they are God-given, and He expects us to use them for His purpose.

This is about Him chiseling away at your character as He works to change you into who He made you to be. The journey is what it's all about, not the great works you do for Him. He doesn't need you, remember; He just wants you to be a part of what He is doing, and He truly cares about how you finish the race called life.

THE TAKEAWAY

God has given you all the abilities and resources necessary to serve His purpose for your life. The question is, what have you done with them? God wants an account. The only wrong answers are, "I didn't do anything" or "I worked on my own castle with those talents."

What is one talent you were born with?

Name one spiritual gift God gave you when you became a believer.

In what way(s) are you putting your talents and gifts to use in the church or the world around you?

CHAPTER 10

Creation

"By the word of the Lord the heavens were made and by the breath of His mouth all their host. He gathers the waters of the sea as a heap; He puts the deeps in the storehouses. Let all the earth fear the Lord; let all the inhabitants of the world stand in awe of Him! For He spoke, and it came to be; He commanded, and it stood firm."—Psalm 33:6-9

It may surprise you to see creation listed in this book, but God's creation is an integral part of a discussion around stewardship, and we need to be reminded of our responsibility to take care of it. In the absence of protecting and preserving His creation, we seem to default to abusing it and destroying it.

Essentially, it's no different now than when God placed Adam and Eve in the Garden of Eden and instructed Adam to "tend and keep it." (Genesis 2:15) In Genesis chapter one, He gave a similar charge to both Adam and Eve: "Be fruitful and increase in number; fill the earth and subdue it. Rule over the fish in the sea and the birds in the sky and over every living creature that moves on the ground." (Genesis 1:28)

Recently, it dawned on me that when I was a kid, by November and December, my friends and I would be skating on frozen lakes. Now, we're lucky if we can skate by mid-January. This winter, 2021, is the first time in my life that our lakes where I live will not be frozen enough to skate on. Whatever the cause, the climate seems to be raging against us. The Sahara Desert is expanding. Deforestation of the Amazon rainforest continues unabated. Hundreds of plant and animal species have been lost to extinction, and thousands more are at risk.

Take the American bison, for example. These great beasts once roamed almost all of North America. When white settlers first arrived, the bison's range extended from the western plains to the Blue Ridge Mountains, swept around to the coastal plains down to Northern Florida, and up to the Carolinas. They numbered in the millions but were slaughtered into near extinction in the 1800s by hunters who sold the hides for a few dollars each. It's said that during 1871 and 1872, an average of five thousand bison were killed every day as thousands of hunters poured onto the western plains. The slaughter continued until 1889 when only about eighty-five free-ranging bison remained.

What a tragedy, especially when one considers that these amazing animals were also critical to the Native Americans who depended on them for every single aspect of their lives. I can't help but wonder the grief God must have felt over the money sickness that led to the expansion of the west on both sides of the U.S. and Canadian border.

Creation loses ground each year as the growth of the planet's population surges. In 1800, five hundred million people were living on earth. By 1900, that number had risen to one billion. In 1919, the year the Spanish Flu struck, the population was one and half billion, and from 1920 to now, the number has swelled to over seven billion. By 2050, researchers say ten billion people will inhabit the planet, with two thirds of that growth on the African continent alone.

Human life is precious, but so is God's creation. And mankind has chosen money over creation since the dawn of time. As Christians, I believe we are called to protect His creation. His Word indeed points to that. Creation is a sign of His existence. Psalm 19:1 says, "The heavens declare the glory of God, and the sky above proclaims His handiwork." Psalm 104:24-25 says, "How many are your works, Lord! In wisdom you made them all; the earth is full of your creatures. There is the sea, vast and spacious, teeming with creatures beyond number — living things both large and small." Is it any wonder that men who reject a Heavenly Creator would choose to destroy His creation? No, but God tasks believers with greater responsibility.

William Wilberforce, recounting in his memoir about the day he became a Christian, Easter Sunday 1786, wrote, "amidst the general chorus with which all nature seems on such a morning to be swelling the song of praise and thanksgiving."

Like Wilberforce, when the Holy Spirit is infused in our lives, we gain a more profound sense of appreciation for God's creation. But with that appreciation should come a grieving in our spirit when we see what humanity is doing to it, often in the pursuit of money, self-interest, fear, or rejection of God's sovereignty. We can excuse ourselves, saying, "I'm not the one doing that." Still, as stewards of what God has entrusted us with, we each have an element of accountability.

PICTURES OF CREATION FROM JONATHAN'S TRAVELS

Lessons Learned from a Three-legged Dog

"You can't buy love but you can rescue it"—Sara Lewis

My wife Sara was the one who truly opened my eyes to our need to steward creation. It all happened courtesy of a small, eight-year-old, three-legged canine with health issues named, of all things, Jaew Borng. (He is named after a spicy chili dip from Thailand.) Let me explain.

One of the organizations we support is the nonprofit *Soi Dog Foundation*, Southeast Asia's largest rescue organization for vulnerable street dogs and stray cats. Along with spay and neuter programs, rescue and treatment, education within schools, and adopting the animals to loving homes overseas, they have also made an enormous dent in helping to eradicate the dog meat trade in Asia. This trade is one of the most serious animal welfare issues in Asia and comes with terrible cruelty and barbaric practices, for us, a senseless inhumane act against God's creatures.

When Sara began talking about adopting one of their dogs, I strongly objected. I remember thinking that if it's not an orphanage in Guatemala, a school in Africa, or the local abortion clinic, something that benefits humans, it's not good stewardship of our resources. "It's certainly not worth throwing away money that God entrusted us with toward rescuing a dog in a shelter in Asia! I mean, come on, honey!" I said one night.

I can say the worst fight of our marriage, and there have not been many, was over this dog. Sara was angry at my obtuse, dismissive response. Eventually, I had a change of heart because a) I realized those animals were God's creatures, and b) my wife gave me no choice. We were getting a dog from Thailand! So, we forked over a decent amount of money to adopt and transport Jaew Borng, our little chili dish, from Thailand to Nova Scotia, where he could be loved and have a home to live out the rest of his life. Four years later, I continue to be amazed at the appreciation for God's creation our kids have come to have just by adopting this dog. Jaew Borng has been an unbelievable blessing to our family. I can honestly say it was money well invested!

I thought about this some more while writing this chapter. It dawned on me, so many people will go to a breeder and buy a purebred dog, whatever breed happens to be the most popular at the moment, or they pay big bucks for "hypoallergenic" or a particular color or size. They will spend thousands of dollars to "get what they want." The dog is another piece of property. They aren't looking for what God would have them do; they look for what they think will make them happy.

It seems like a small, simple life choice, but is it? Ironically, I would have fallen into that category and missed out on being a part of seeing one of God's creatures being rescued had I persevered and resisted my wife's fury. Our kids have been a part of living with and loving a creature they know we saved, not one we bought.

It's pretty powerful if you think about it. Imagine the love this little guy gets. I guarantee you he thinks he has already died and gone to heaven. And, thankfully, my wife didn't have to kill me and send me on early.

Standing in the Gap for God's Greatest Creation

Earlier in the book, I introduced the concept of justice as a critical element of stewardship. That applies to creation as well.

The Bible tells us to stand for what is just where no one else will. It explains justice as God defines it, not in humanity's terms. Isaiah 1:17 puts it succinctly: "Learn to do good; seek justice, correct oppression; bring justice to the fatherless, plead the widow's cause." Proverbs 31:8-9 says, "Open your mouth for the mute, for the rights of all who are destitute. Open your mouth, judge righteously, defend the rights of the poor and needy."

God's definition of justice never changes (Deuteronomy 32:4; Psalm 89:14), while man's definition (social justice) is constantly changing. Please don't confuse the two. They are not always the same, even if they parallel each other occasionally.

Like everything we have explored so far, it is important to note that I'm focused on God's will for our lives and not our own. Like everything we have discussed on stewardship, we have to decide whether we are stewards of His justice or our flawed interpretation as influenced by our worldview. So, when considering God's will for His creation, we don't have a right to impose our will here any more than over any other part of our lives.

God tells us to stand in the gap for the weak. "Religion that is pure and undefiled before God, the Father, is this: to visit orphans and widows in their affliction and to keep oneself unstained from the world." (James 1:27) In 1 John 3:17, the Bible tells us life is precious and to fight for it. As Christians, we need to be resolute in our stand for God's most incredible creation, human life in the form of the unborn.

In Psalm 139:13-16, the writer, King David, states, "For you formed my inward parts; you knitted me together in my mother's womb. I praise you, for I am fearfully and wonderfully made. Wonderful are your works; my soul knows it very well. My frame was not hidden from you, when I was being made in secret, intricately woven in the depths of the earth. Your eyes saw my unformed substance; in your book were written, every one of them, the days that were formed for me, when as yet there was none of them."

We know from modern science that an unborn child has dreams, can feel pain, and senses their environment. They have feelings and play in the womb. They are living human beings who are, for a time, dependent on their mothers for survival. However, they are not part of their mother's body but distinct and separate creations with a unique genetic code and heartbeat.

If we are serious about being stewards of creation, we must fight for the unborn and combat the scourge on humanity called abortion. God's justice demands it.

In the nearly fifty years since being legalized in the U.S., abortion has cost the lives of close to forty-five million infants. In New York City, there are more black babies aborted each year than are born. Abortion is the leading cause of death worldwide. Sex-selective abortions are common globally. In Asia, one hundred sixty million women are missing today due to sex-selective abortions. That is equivalent to nearly the entire female population of the United States. Just as two hundred years ago, slavery was a stain on that generation and all the generations before, so is murdering an unborn child today a stain on ours.

William Wilberforce took an unpopular stand because God demanded it of him. Today, we are faced with a similar requirement. Are we going to stand up for the murder of unborn children because they are undesired? Are we prepared to open our hearts and make a home for a child if need be?

We may not be able to prevent what is happening to the planet and God's most incredible creation at the hands of mankind. Still, we can fight for it with grace and love, and by "putting skin in the game," and offer an alternative. We may be limited in the influence we can have in preserving what He has made, but we are called to try.

Now you may struggle with what I said or that I would dare to voice a position on this sensitive topic given that I am a man. But stewarding justice on behalf of the unborn is the responsibility of all God's people. I could not call myself a Christian were I not clear and unwavering on what His Word says about His greatest creation, human life.

Our Own Creation Stewardship Struggle

In our mid-thirties, Sara and I prayerfully decided to have a family together. We were raising two daughters part-time from my previous marriage, but were eager to start a family ourselves.

We had difficulty from the word go. We could not conceive, and it dealt us both an emotional blow. Sara loved her step-daughters, but we wanted a family unit that wasn't divided and the harmony of not having kids who had to go back and forth between two homes with very different worldviews.

Sara and I struggled with whether this was God's will for us and how far we would go to conceive. We contemplated adoption. For a season, Sara researched our options at great length but we decided to try in-vitro fertilization (IVF) first.

We prayed for God's guidance every step of the way. We kept saying, "Lord, we want your will, not our own. If it is not your will that we have children together, give us the courage to accept that. If it is, remove the roadblocks and help us conceive."

We agreed we would only go so far with science and then give it to God. For something we wanted so desperately, the thought of drawing a line and accepting that perhaps it wasn't His will was very, very difficult. It came with many tears and long walks asking why, but we finally agreed to stop at the point of freezing a fertilized egg.

Some of you might say we went too far playing God and not trusting His sovereignty. Others might say if we had gotten that far to keep going. Our feeling was that if we couldn't successfully put a fertilized egg in Sara's womb and have a life spring forth, then we had to accept we were at an impasse, and our inability to conceive might be His answer.

Could we have kept going? Yes. Were there more options available to us? Yes. But, through the IVF process, discovering there was no apparent reason medically or otherwise why we couldn't conceive naturally, we agreed to take a breather and accept that maybe we were caught up in the world's view of playing God with life.

In our case, it wasn't in the context of aborting an unwanted baby but of *wanting* a baby. However, the desire stemmed from the same place: self — what we wanted versus God's will for us. We had to wrestle with how far we were prepared to go to get what we wanted and at what point we would let go and trust Him.

As you can see, although I can't speak from experience about abortion personally, I can about surrender of my will to His in a very sensitive area that hits close to home but on the opposite side of the spectrum. The chapter isn't closed on this part of our life, but we trust Him for answers and direction, not our desires and impulses.

In the meantime, we are blessed with two amazing young women, Maddy and Clara, ages thirteen and fifteen, respectively. They are a joy to influence and lead to a deeper understanding of God. And we support the local crisis pregnancy center in our city with our time, talent, and finances.

Our Family and Creation

Sara and I planned to have our own kids, and once they were grown, build a boat and sail away. Sounds romantic, but we both agreed it was a pipe dream where we would have gone down a path of manipulating our surroundings to manufacture happiness. It was about having control and not trusting God.

Instead, in faith, we are filled with joy as our marriage flourishes, and we grow deeper in our understanding of God and each other. There is a peace that comes from letting go and "rolling with the punches" of life, thanking Him for the good things He blesses us with instead of the scarcity mindset that's always longing for more, never fully satisfied.

We are at peace as we make our way through our days, no matter what life throws at us. Why? Because we trust God even if we didn't get what we wanted or the answer we expected. Even if, in His providence, we aren't meant to parent any other children than our girls, we have the sense that we are exactly where He wants us. And that is enough.

In 2020, thanks to the Covid-19 pandemic, like everyone

else, we found ourselves with more time on our hands than we expected. Since we couldn't attend church, we took hikes on Sunday mornings instead.

It's incredible what a six-kilometer hike along the Nova Scotian coast, sitting down together to have a sandwich on an eighty-foot bluff overlooking the Atlantic Ocean can do for the soul. With the sun on our face and wind in our hair our family took church in God's cathedral. We would pick out a biblical theme to discuss on each hike, something that pointed us to our Creator.

We would spend this time Sunday after Sunday outside and were reminded of Psalm 19:1, which says, "The heavens declare the glory of God, and the sky above proclaims His handiwork." One particular Sunday, we even discussed stewardship — which was more important, money or time? That was the question I asked the girls. That's also when I felt the Lord leading me to write this book.

I can't help but wonder if I would have gotten such a deep desire to know God's will surrounding stewardship if it had not been for the journey our family went through together during the long months of Covid. (I think the answer is no.) But as I sat on a bluff overlooking the Atlantic that Sunday morning listening to my wife read the Bible to Maddy and Clara, I knew it was God's will that we were sitting where we were at that very moment.

PICTURES OF FAMILY HIKES

Steps to Stewarding Creation

In many of these chapters, we list a series of action steps to help you, the reader, start on a particular aspect of your stewardship journey. In this chapter, there are four I recommend:

- Get out in creation, enjoy it, and remind yourself how beautiful it really is.
- Like Adam and Eve, who God charged with tending the garden, do your part to protect His creation. Until God creates a new heaven and new earth, it's the only one we have.
- As a Christian, ask God how you can use your influence in the battle for the family unit. Be it as a Big Brother or Big Sister, volunteering at a crisis pregnancy center, adopting a child who desperately needs your love and protection — or adopting a three-legged dog from the other side of the planet. There are many ways you can steward God's creation.
- Watch Louie Giglio's sermon, Pale Blue Dot, on YouTube: https://youtu.be/6-qxALLb61Mik.

THE TAKEAWAY

Enjoying and caring for God's creation is one aspect of holistic stewardship. Often, the greatest injustices are being perpetrated against His creation, including His greatest creation, human life in the unborn form. This is a frontline battle the church must fight, so make it a point to do your part.

Does it surprise you that creation is on the list of things we are to steward?

What is one way you can steward God's creation?

What are your views on abortion? If pro-life, what do you see as your responsibility to fight for the unborn?

CHAPTER 11

Money

"A strange species we are, we can stand anything God and nature can throw at us save only plenty. If I wanted to destroy a nation, I would give it too much, and I would have it on its knees, miserable, greedy, sick."—John Steinbeck

"The earth is the Lords and everything in it."
—1 Corinthians 10:26 (That includes your money!)

"Nevertheless man, though in honor, does not remain: He is like the beasts that perish."—Psalm 49:12

"Surely every man walks about like a shadow: Surely they busy themselves in vain: He heaps up riches and does not know who will gather them."—Psalm 39:6

Did you know that Jesus spent more time talking about money than heaven or hell combined? Why? Because this medium of exchange can so easily become an idol in our lives. Jesus knew that and told His disciples no one can serve two masters, God and money. The moment that acquiring money becomes your life's focal point, Jesus has lost you. He wants you to go from a closed fist to an open hand and from a scarcity mindset to one of plenty. That doesn't mean you will have plenty. It means He will provide if you step out in faith and give.

In Matthew 6:26-30, He challenges our faith, asking us why we worry over material possessions.

"Look at the birds of the air; they do not sow or reap or store away in barns, and yet your heavenly Father feeds them.... See how the flowers of the field grow. They do not labor or spin. Yet I tell you that not even Solomon in all his splendor was dressed like one of these."

"Try me and see if I won't provide" is his invitation. (Malachi 3:10)

The Ten Percent Glass Ceiling

The church has created a religious framework that says, take ten percent, give it to the Lord, and by default everything else is yours. That mindset borders on heresy. The truth is that one hundred percent of it is His. Ten percent is the starting point, not the endpoint.

God knows we need money to live. He also knows it's a measurement of our time. Because you are flesh and bone, you're limited by time in how much of this resource you can attain. It's different for each of us — some acquire more and some less.

God is interested in your willingness to acknowledge that none of it is yours.

Whether you're a professional football player like Kirk Cousins with a twenty-four-million-dollar a year contract or a janitor who cleans up the stadium after the game, the payment you receive isn't yours; it's His.

What God is looking for is not a person who gives ten percent and pats himself on the back, but someone who says it's one hundred percent His and is obedient with it. Like the widow's mite, He would much rather have the janitor who has a one hundred percent mindset than the wealthy athlete who gives ten percent of his twenty-four million. One gets it, and the other doesn't.

That's why He zeroed in on the rich young ruler (Matthew 19:16–30, Mark 10:17–31, Luke 18:18–30), where Jesus said, "You lack one thing. Go and sell everything you have and give it to the poor."

Why was that His instruction? Because Jesus knew the only thing that would keep the young ruler out of heaven was his love of money. Jesus could have just as easily been talking to the janitor who also had a love of money, even if he didn't have any, and instructed the same thing. It's being possessed by the love of money, not possessing it, that is the threat.

Not everyone needs to sell all they have and give to the poor. It's about the state of our heart around money. If we have an open hand, we surrender His money to Him and then let Him decide what He wants us to do with it. Once we surrender, it won't matter, whatever His decision.

If there's one reason to write this book, it's to challenge Christians to ask, have you put God in a box when it comes to money, or do you truly understand that it all belongs to Him and you have your part to play? If every believer were to do that, we would have more than enough resources to fulfill the Great Commission right now.

The Trouble with the Tithe

The tithe is a benchmark the church created to give people a standard to which they can aspire. The Bible provides loose guidance. The prophet Malachi said to bring all the tithes into the storehouse. (Malachi 3:8-12) In Genesis 14:20, Abram gave Melchizedek a tenth of all the goods he had recovered.

But the tithe can be a slippery slope because it creates a legalistic mindset around money very easily for those who want a checklist instead of a heart examination. The moment we establish a fixed amount, we dictate the terms, not God. We struggle to pry open a closed fist instead of opening our hand and trusting Him with what is already His. We get ninety percent, and He gets ten. How does that measure up with the concept of holistic stewardship? It doesn't.

I remember watching an interview with Bill Bright, founder of Campus Crusade for Christ, and Vonette, his wife. They referenced the reverse tithe, giving away ninety percent of their earnings and living on ten. Watch the full interview here https://www.youtube.com/watch?v=w1kutOlR8fo.

In that interview, Bright said, "All that you possess is really His, and you are entrusted as a steward. If you have more than you need to live, give it all away to help fulfill the Great Commission. ... When we get to heaven, [the question] is not going to be 'how much money did you make,' but how faithful were you with what I called you to do?" To that, his wife Vonette added, "Use what you have, whether it's little or much, to honor God. He takes care of everything else."

I have to tell you, that idea both floored and scared me. I had never heard of a reverse tithe or even knew it was a possibility, and... I wanted to do it. In my heart, I was like, "Lord, that is scary and at the same time sounds really, really awesome. I'd like to be able to do that with what you have entrusted me, Lord."

However, at the time, I wasn't giving ten percent. You heard me correctly. Sara and I were only giving about three percent. I hadn't thought much about it, to be honest. Ignorantly, I was giving out of comfort rather than conviction. I was definitely in the "I'm blessed camp." I didn't realize what kind of accountability would be expected of me with what we had been "blessed."

It had yet to dawn on me that God, the creator of the universe, could connect with me through giving. I couldn't see how God cared about money or what I gave or did not give in His desire to be in a relationship with me.

After listening to the interview with Bill and Vonette, I started reading more about what the Bible said about money. I learned that God gives us our place in the world and a free will to choose Him or the idol of *self* and then waits to see what we will do with that free will and the resources He has entrusted to us.

There we were, Sara and I, living more for ourselves. The Lord began convicting me about our spending habits.

I shared my convictions with Sara, and we started to make changes. We submitted to the leadership of a good friend, Lorne Robinson, the chair for Kingdom Advisors Canada. We began paying down our debt while, at the same time, increasing our giving. We set a goal of ten percent within two years.

Although Sara and I didn't talk about it in great detail, we both knew we weren't planning on stopping at ten percent. Still, I needed to prove to myself, Sara, and God that I could do the basics before I knew the Lord would take the stewardship training wheels off and give us a push.

During that time, we paid off all our debt. We cruised towards ten percent, and I have to tell you, it felt amazing. We were content. No longer did we yearn for more stuff. Then the first test came.

In the fall of 2019, we had retired our debt and were giving about eight percent. Sara and I had made a verbal commitment to Lorne that we would increase our giving again in April of 2020. This would be a significant increase all at once, and I was stressing about it a bit. But I was resolute that we were pressing forward in faith. However, in March 2020, along came Covid.

My profession is wealth management, where I manage people's money for a living. There I was in February 2020, and things were humming. I was taking precautions for my clients as it seemed a market correction was looming, but I certainly wasn't prepared for the hit we took in March and April.

I had just hired a new COO, Matt Jenkinson, to step in and help me run the company. He signed his employment letter on February 26, the same day as the first big market drop in response to the Covid pandemic. Fast forward to his start date on April 14, and the equivalent of his annual income had been wiped out and more by market losses on my block of business.

I was also committed to increasing my giving by a little more than two percent starting that same month. "Two percent of what," I said to the Lord prayerfully. "My income and that of my employees is in jeopardy, and I have a new guy starting I can't afford." I felt the Holy Spirit say, "Jonathan, try me."

I told my controller, Katie, to take our personal giving to where I had planned before the pandemic. Matt took a leap of faith and joined our company, leaving a secure job, even though I told him where things stood. He is a believer and was so bold to say, "I'm coming over as planned, and we will figure it out together." What happened next is amazing.

The year before, I had let several advisors go. They weren't performing, and apart from our top-line income, there was no real impact on our firm. I did this with trepidation but felt the Holy Spirit leading me in a specific direction regarding the firm's culture.

A year later, in March through August of 2020, in response to Covid, the Canadian Federal Government rolled out economic stimulus programs based on your previous year's gross business income. Your business needed to be down a certain amount year-over-year to qualify. And wouldn't you know it, we qualified because I had let those employees go. What we collected was half of Matt's salary for the year. By the time we no longer qualified, we were back on our feet, no worse for wear, and Sara and I were more than able to make our giving commitment. God said, "Try me." I did, and He showed up.

It became crystal clear to me that we can't outgive God. He wants to mature us through the journey of giving and the surrender of our lives to Him. Money stewardship is a tool he uses to shape us and cultivate our spiritual character. I couldn't help but think about the Lord's Prayer and how Jesus said, "Give us this day our daily bread."

When it comes to biblical stewardship, we have to answer the question of who owns it. If we are saved by grace through faith and say the reason for our entire existence is to glorify God, except where it comes to our money, financially, we're putting God in a box. We are saying, "He is not Lord of all, only Lord of my life up to ten percent of *my* liquid resources." The moment we accept the notion that ten percent is satisfactory, we have effectively removed God's lordship over the other ninety — the exact opposite of Bill Bright's decision concerning his finances.

Money Reflects our Heart's Condition

We can fake everything else in the Christian walk except for how we handle money; it's measurable. That's the big difference. We can see what each of us does with our money. If you're only giving one percent of your income, that demonstrates your mindset. Why only one percent? The chances are you are spending too much on lifestyle, taxes, and debt repayment.

You can't control tax rates; the government sets those. But if your lifestyle is too opulent, it creates debt. People use debt to fund their lifestyle, and debt fosters an environment where you have no money to give or save. What does the Bible teach? Spend less than we earn and avoid debt, especially consumer debt driven by fleshly desire.

1 John 2:16 says, "For all that is in the world — the desires of the flesh and the desires of the eyes, and the pride of life — is not from the Father but from the world." We buy things we can't afford. It's an internal dialogue we're not having and need to have with ourselves, our spouse, and God. As humorist Will Rogers put it, "Too many people spend money they don't have to buy things they don't need to impress people they don't like."

In the meantime, giving suffers because we go into a downward mental spiral of scarcity rather than abundance. Our overconsumption reveals our heart's condition. Christian financial advisor Ron Blue said, "Show me what you do with your money, and I'll show you where your heart is." Meanwhile, giving breaks the hold money has on your heart.

In his classic bestseller, *The Cross and the Switchblade*, pastor and author David Wilkerson used the example of a dog with a bone to describe how to win people to Christ. That example is just as applicable to giving.

"You see a dog passing down the street with an old bone in his mouth. You don't grab the bone from him and tell him it's not good for him. He'll growl at you. It's the only thing he has. But you throw a big fat lamb chop in front of him, and he's going to drop that bone and pick up the lamb chop, his tail wagging to beat the band."

The kingdom of God is like that fat lamb chop. It brings contentment, peace, joy, satisfaction in and with God alone. It's what my wife and I keep discovering as we aggressively engage in stewardship, sowing into people's lives with our time, money, and talents.

The one-verse parable, Matthew 13:44, says, "The kingdom of heaven is like treasure hidden in a field, which a man found and covered up. Then in his joy he goes and sells all that he has and buys that field."

I pray that the church would wake up and stop holding on to an old bone. God will exchange it for a "lamb chop." It may not be more money, however. It could be peace on the home front where you never thought peace would come or a friendship you so desperately need. But the Word promises that we can't outgive

God. He will show up in powerful ways suited perfectly to you.

Luke 6:38 says, "He will pour into your lap a good measure — pressed down, shaken together, and running over. For by your standard of measure, it will be measured to you in return." This applies to all parts of stewardship, from friendships to how we invest our time, money, and other resources. He will pour into you if you give holistically, out of a generous heart, with all that He has entrusted you.

But as 2 Corinthians 9:6-8 states, "Whoever sows sparingly will also reap sparingly, and whoever sows bountifully will also reap bountifully. Each one must give as he has decided in his *heart*, not reluctantly or under compulsion, for God loves a cheerful giver. And God is able to make all grace abound to you so that having all sufficiency in all things at all times, you may abound in every good work."

Our Need to Learn Contentment

The response to our misuse of God's financial resources needs to be repentance, where we ask the Lord to help us learn contentment. Not unlike the struggle Sara and I had in starting our own family. We had to come to a place of truly being content, whether God enabled us to conceive or not.

Contentment is not a character trait we're born with; we have to learn it. The Apostle Paul said in Philippians 4:11, "I have learned to be content in whatever circumstances I am." To his protégé, Timothy, he said, "Godliness with contentment is great gain." (I Timothy 6:6)

As good stewards, we should pursue contentment, spend less than we earn, pay down our debt, and treat God's resources with the respect they deserve by giving them away for kingdom building. We have to start where we are and move upward. If you're at one percent, make it your goal to get to three percent. If at ten percent, then thirty, and so forth. The amount doesn't matter after a while. Why? Because you found something unseen that is much, much better. The ultimate goal is to get to a place of absolute surrender. God will decide how much our time is worth and how much we can earn. What we must decide is whether we will be open-handed or close-fisted with what He has entrusted us. Will we trust Him that He has even better things in store?

Steps to Money Stewardship

Pursue Contentment

As indicated above, the first step in properly stewarding God's money is to learn contentment. When it comes to financial decisions, are we content or discontent? For the vast majority of people living in North America, the necessary amenities — food, clothing, shelter — are taken care of. From Maslow's Hierarchy of Needs perspective, we need nothing, so for most of us, it's all want.

Ask, am I pursuing contentment and being mindful of what I have? Plenty of scriptures confirm the reasons to do this.

"Command those who are rich in this present world not to be arrogant nor to put their hope in wealth, which is so uncertain, but to put their hope in God, who richly provides us with everything for our enjoyment." I Timothy 6:17

"I have learned the secret of being content in any and every situation, whether well-fed or hungry, whether living in plenty or in want. I can do everything through Him who gives me strength." Philippians 4:11-13

"Keep your lives free from the love of money and be content with what you have." Hebrews 13:5

"Do not love the world or anything in the world. If anyone loves the world, love for the Father is not in them." 1 John 2:5

"Make it your ambition to lead a quiet life: You should mind your own business and work with your hands, just as we told you, so that your daily life may win the respect of outsiders and so that you will not be dependent on anybody." I Thessalonians 4:11-12

Think with Eternity in View

I'm not talking about storing up treasure in heaven. I am talking about the journey of sanctification, the "great adventure," to quote singer-songwriter, Steven Curtis Chapman. Why would we want to put God in a box with our money when we can keep maturing in our faith regardless of which side of eternity we are on?

Talk to God About Your Finances

God wants to talk to us about our money, to dialog about His resources and how to manage them. We come to a dead stop if money gets in the way of that relationship through our unwillingness to acknowledge His lordship over it. There are no independent financial choices; they are all either with God in mind or our selfish desires in mind.

Put Your Financial House in Order

Pay down your debt, spend less than you earn, change your

lifestyle as needed so you can give more and save more. It's a virtuous cycle.

Step Out in Faith

We all need to step out in faith for many reasons. Doing so with our giving allows God to demonstrate that He will honor our willingness to glorify Him. It often creates an environment where our faith will be tested, and He has the opportunity to show up. It's when the possible slips over into the impossible, and God gets to flex His muscles to show us what is possible through Him.

Conclusion

In chapter three, I talked about the encounter with my pastors over stewardship of money, a resource I had in abundance and desperately wanted to know how to use for kingdom purposes. Their advice: commit to tithing. Years later, I reached out to Lorne Robinson. His counsel was quite different. He taught me an essential lesson, one that is the main thread running through this book: God owns it all.

He gave me a simple formula that I have tried to follow since then. He said if you pay off debt, you won't need as much income. If you take less income from your business, you pay fewer taxes. If you give and save, you also save on taxes and have more for your lifestyle. It's that simple.

When I embraced His counsel and started giving, it set me free from the love of money. It broke the power money had over me. What is amazing, as Sara and I were willing to free up resources to further God's kingdom, increasingly our calling has become more and more self-evident.

No longer do we wonder where God wants us to go or what to do because we're doing it daily, and He is leading with each step. His Word is the lamp to our feet, and our feet are moving. The fruit of that is events like the annual turkey drive we organize every Christmas, our support of Teen Challenge, and the giving we do as a family through the non-profit family foundation we started ten years ago.

Society tells us that the more we have, the more important we are, that our self-worth is tied to our net worth. Therefore, we seek to acquire as much wealth as we can. Generous giving flies in the face of that and releases the hold money has over us. It also breaks the power of self. You can't be selfish if you're giving it all away. That's a lesson Bill Bright learned. So did Lorne Robinson, who passed it on to me, and I'm now passing it along to you. Remember, God owns it all. You can either respond with a closed fist or open hand. The decision is yours.

THE TAKEAWAY

How you handle money reflects your heart's condition. You have to believe and accept that it all belongs to God and honor Him through generous giving.

What impact does the phrase "God owns it all" have on your view of money?

Does spending on your lifestyle keep you from giving? What changes can you make with your household spending to give more?

What benefits have you experienced by giving generously?

CHAPTER 12

God's Scandalous Grace

"You can cut me up into a thousand pieces and lay them in the street, and every piece will still love you."
—David Wilkerson to Nicky Cruise
(*The Cross and the Switchblade*)

God gave us two gifts we don't deserve, grace and forgiveness. Grace is scandalous if you think about it. We live in a world where we have a wage mentality. We receive rewards for actions. But Jesus models something so different. He gives us His grace as the ultimate act of stewardship for nothing in return other than an offer to accept it.

A stumbling block for many believers is that God's grace hasn't transformed them. They long for it. They get it intellectually but can't give it. Why? How does someone like David Wilkerson, founder of Teen Challenge, when faced with a switchblade to his face, say loving words to a gang leader bent on killing him? Because God's amazing grace gripped him.

As I have grown and matured in my faith, I have discovered that the currency of heaven is grace. Looking back, Matthew 13:44, the passage about finding a treasure in a field was jarring for me. The Holy Spirit was showing me something infinitely more valuable than what I had been pursuing my entire life, and it was the very thing from which I had been running. Now I wanted to buy that field! But how? I was still trapped in a transactional understanding of God.

I struggled with forgiveness for years. I knew we are called to forgive as Christians, but that was easier said than done. I would angrily pray to God over some offense or ongoing abuse and ask, "How? How do I forgive?" I'd quote Matthew 18:21 to Jesus (as if He needed reminding) where Peter asked how many times we should forgive someone. Jesus' reply, "not seven times but seventy times seven."

It made me angry. "He didn't say HOW! I would growl. What if you're at two thousand times? Then what, Lord?" Then one day, it hit me. The Spirit graciously posed the question during a walk. "Jonathan, how can you withhold your grace and forgiveness when you have received mine? You don't have that right if you truly understand what I did for you and everyone who is lost. If you love me, then the *how* is out of love for me, obedience to me, and a desire to glorify me."

I didn't hear God speak audibly, just the Spirit's still, small voice in my heart and mind. That was the beginning of answering the *how*. He had me. His grace overwhelmed me, and I realized how trivial the things I was holding onto, were in light of eternity. A load was lifted from me in an instant. I saw the things of this world in a much smaller frame and the things of God in a much larger one, and I knew I had to faithfully steward His grace to everyone I met.

Peter Receives Christ's Scandalous Grace

Ryan Walter, a good friend of mine, pointed me to John 21:20-25 while we were discussing Jesus' grace. The passage was a fresh reminder of how patient Jesus is with us and the magnitude of His grace. You could easily miss it, but after Jesus reinstates Peter and calls him to feed and love his sheep and the lost, Peter shows his flesh. Perhaps he was still feeling deep conviction over his sinful acts of denial before Jesus' crucifixion. But in verse twenty-one, he asks, "What about him?" referring to John. Peter wanted to redirect Jesus' attention away.

Isn't that like us? Jesus will wrestle with us, and rather than own our shortcomings, we deflect, redirect, and even defend ourselves. Peter was missing the amazing grace Jesus was showing him in that very moment. (I can relate.)

What a "numpty" Peter was early on. Thankfully, Jesus chipped away at Peter's character, and, as believers, we are the better for it because of the letters he wrote. Peter grew to truly understand that we are but beggars lost in search of heavenly bread, who, in the end, need to eagerly share where we found it by demonstrating it in our lives to others.

The Prodigal Son and God's Scandalous Grace

The Parable of the Prodigal Son, as told in Luke 15:11-32, is another example of God's scandalous grace.

There are three characters in this story: the father (who represents our heavenly Father), the young son who left home to seek the world's pleasures (representative of lost humanity), and the elder son who stayed to serve his father (representative of legalistic believers).

I won't delve into the passage too deeply except to suggest this: The son who never left felt jaded when his wayward brother returned. He found himself confronted with but did not comprehend the scandalous grace his father showed his brother.

In Luke 15:25, the Bible says, "Now his older son was in the field (working hard, we can assume, for the father), and as he came and drew near to the house, he heard music and dancing." Verse twenty-eight says, "But he was angry and refused to go in."

Then, in verse twenty-nine, he rebukes his father, "Look, these many years I have served you, and never disobeyed your command; yet you never gave me a young goat, that I might celebrate with my friends. But when this son of yours, who has devoured your property with prostitutes, came, you killed the fattened calf for him!"

He failed to see the amazing grace demonstrated by the father, who, in celebrating his son's return, joyfully replied, "For this, your brother was dead, and is alive; he was lost and is found."

The Church's Prodigal Grace

I think the church most often is like the elder son.

David Seamands, an evangelical Christian counselor and author, summed up his career this way:

"Many years ago, I was driven to the conclusion that the two major causes of most emotional problems among evangelical

Christians are these: the failure to understand, receive, and live out God's unconditional grace and forgiveness; and the failure to give out that unconditional love, forgiveness, and grace to other people… We read, we hear, we believe a good theology of grace. But that is not the way we live. The good news of the Gospel of grace has not penetrated the level of our emotions."

Now you might be reading this and say, Jonathan you are generalizing here. The church as a whole isn't all like the elder son in the parable. I agree. I have met many believers who demonstrated amazing grace to me personally despite my apparent sin and shortcomings. Some I mentioned already in this book. But if we're being honest, I think we can agree that there are many who are not good stewards of God's grace to the world. And I have to wonder if they really get it? If they did, then they would ask how can we not forgive those who have offended us? How can we not welcome the lost in droves into our churches? We should be chasing after them. Why are we hoarding His grace? Why do the lost feel safe with Jesus and not with His church? Why are we sowing judgment more often than grace into relationships, even among fellow believers? Could it be because we are like the older son? We have many churches who wouldn't know where to start in loving, receiving and fighting for the LGBTQ, or the woman who aborted her child, or the man addicted to porn, the adulterers and alcoholics who come in and sit in the back of the church. Let's be brutally honest, they aren't coming in and sitting in the back of the church. They would rather be anywhere but near a church where they would experience judgement and condemnation.

I know that was me when I wasn't a Christian and it is often the first thing out of the mouth of someone who has had no or little interaction with the "church." Let's face it, the world has us pegged and it isn't with the peg of grace. Grace is the key. If we don't get it, we won't demonstrate it. If we don't demonstrate it, then the church is nothing more than a community center for morally self-righteous people to hang out. Once we wrestle with God's grace and truly realize we were and are sinners saved by grace just like the rest of the world, then it is easy to answer the question of, now what?

Understanding God's scandalous grace lead me to ask, how can I not plow into the world to share the good news that Jesus came to set the captives free? As stewards, we shouldn't be seasoning our conversations with grace; we should be drowning them in it. It is the one thing all of humanity craves desperately and we give out so little of it to each other. Why?

THE TAKEAWAY

God's unconditional grace and forgiveness is the one thing that makes Christianity unique among the world's religions, even if many inside the safety of the church don't get it. The world is desperate for it, and we are to be stewards of it.

What does God's grace mean to you?

What is the most challenging thing you ever had to forgive? Were you able to forgive? If not, how has this exploration of grace helped you?

Who is one person you need to steward grace to?

CHAPTER 13

Relationships

"If you aren't spending time with the Lord every day, you won't have much to give to people in your life."
—Ron Blue

"As iron sharpens iron, so one person sharpens another." Proverbs 27:17

It is safe to say that we can't talk about stewardship without understanding our call to positively and lovingly influence the people around us, pointing them to Jesus. Both Matthew 28:19 and Mark 16:15 state it matter-of-factly: "Go and make disciples."

If relationships are core to a Christian's life and God tells us to share the good news to all nations, love, and show them the same grace and mercy He revealed to us through salvation, then this isn't a grey area.

Relational Stewardship Starts at Home

I often think of relational stewardship from the perspective of where we have the most influence and impact to the least influence and impact. Typically, that starts in the home with our family.

1 Timothy 5:8 rattles in my ear, especially since my daughters are growing up in a broken home with divorced parents. It says, "If anyone does not provide for his relatives, and especially his household, he has denied the faith and is worse than an unbeliever."

Providing for and discipling my family is my number one job and top priority. I need to pour my life into my marriage and my kids and then take care of my extended family. I always think of my vows to Sara in the context of Ephesians 5:25. When that passage says love your wives, just as Christ loved the church... well Jesus died for His bride. So for me, after God, nothing is more important to me than Sara. Then, my focus is on our girls. Earlier I mentioned some of the tools we use as a family as a way of stewarding ourselves. One of my favorites is our "I Like Book."

More than 10 years ago I started sitting my family down at the end of the day and asking each of them, as I recorded it into our "I Like Book," what they liked the most about their day. It could include something someone in the family did for them or how someone in our household encouraged another. It didn't matter. What did matter was that it created a platform to encourage the kids in their walk with Christ and ease into a prayer time before bed. It has been powerful in our home. Sara and I also have taken discipleship very seriously in our home. We haven't relied on the church or others to teach the girls. We have taken that upon ourselves and it takes work. It is rewarding work though and we always learn as much as the kids do by doing it. A recent example of this is when we shared an interview between JD Grear and Rebecca McLaughlin. The interview dove into the LGBTQ dialogue and how the church can and needs to show up in a positive and powerful way today around this most recent social justice epicenter. The interview confronted the homophobic side of the church and helped to unpack it in a constructive way so our girls could continue to be in the world daily as Chrisitians in their school, witnessing the lost world God has placed them in. I couldn't help but think of Dietrich Bonhoeffer's words regarding 1930's Germany when he said, "If you are going to serve Jesus you have to serve the times you live in." Today we are serving a society jockeying for their rights. It doesn't mean they *are* right. But we have concluded as a family we need to wade into this broken world and meet it head on where it is with the same truth, love, and grace as those who have come before us that did it well. We as a family believe the church and Christians need to get on the right side of history when it comes to reaching the lost, unlike the civil rights movements of the 60s and 70s where many in the church failed miserably. As a result, the girls are reading Rebecca's book - *10 Questions Every Teen Should Ask (and Answer) about Christianity.*

We also make a huge effort to ensure our family is interacting with other believers. Not exclusively, but enough to ensure we are getting a healthy dose of Christian fellowship. That is what the church is for - mutual edification. In short, when it comes to stewarding relationships, you have to start at home. The good thing is, it prepares you for the front door.

Proverbs 22:6 says, "Train up a child in the way he should go; even when he is old, he will not depart from it." Ephesians 6:4 instructs fathers to "not provoke your children to anger but bring them up in the discipline and instruction of the Lord." In I Kings 10:8, the Queen of Sheba says concerning Solomon's God-given wisdom, "Happy are your wives."

Like Moses, I am called to teach our family, immediate and extended, to "number their days and grow in wisdom." (Psalm 90:12)

Relational Stewardship Beyond Your Front Door

> "Oh God, make the bad people good, and the good people nice."—Unknown

God puts relationships in our path for a purpose, and we are accountable to Him for how we treat those we encounter. I often think that the Lord put me in this world to serve others and those people somewhere out there have my *name* on them. If they are to hear the good news of Jesus and they are to be set free, it depends on my obedience. Think about it, like my friend Mark in Peru, your stewardship of all you possess; your skills, talents, money and more could have someone's name on it that God is in His divine eternal plan linking to you. He is simply waiting for you to go. Like Jesus, we have to meet people where they are, just as Jesus did when He came across the tax collector, Zacchaeus, perched in a tree, or the Samaritan woman at the well, or Peter and his fellow fishermen by the Sea of Galilee.

Jesus did not browbeat people no matter how He found them.

He showed them grace, love, and mercy instead. He was firm, to the point, and asked a lot of questions in love. People often went away challenged to go deeper. But they also felt safe with Him. Even the scribes and pharisees, with their wicked intentions, afraid of losing power over the people, often went away from an encounter with Jesus perplexed. Some, like Nicodemus, came back, desiring to know more.

As Christians, the question you and I must ask is, "Am I being a good steward of the relationships God has placed in front of me, regardless if they are a believer or not, or am I turning away and hardening my heart when an offense is given?"

The choice is to get our hands dirty and have healthy constructive conflict at times. Other times, it is just letting things go and giving it to God, wading into that relationship because He has called us to it. And at others, we are called to walk away. But even distancing ourselves from some people should always be done in love, not out of malice, pride, or hurt feelings.

People may only be in our lives for a season. It's up to God whether that relationship has ongoing traction or means for us to do life with them more intimately. Either way, we must choose to be an encourager, building them up, or a critic, tearing them down.

We will impact everyone we meet. The question the Lord put to me a few years back is, will it be positive or negative? Will you point them to me or away? He holds us accountable if we turn people away by our selfish behavior.

In Matthew 18:6, Jesus says, "It is better to have a millstone tied around your neck and drowned in the depth of the sea" if you cause a believer to stumble into sin. The fact is, we are all accountable to each other, to spur each other on, and encourage each other through God's Word. My observation in the church today is we resemble the world a lot. We seem more interested in being right than relevant. We don't have surrendered hearts for those we are doing life with. We want to be heard and win rather than be gracious. Often theological correctness trumps loving grace packed with loving truth.

Mark Twain used to say he put a dog and a cat in a cage together as an experiment to see if they could get along. They did, so he put in a bird, pig, and goat. They, too, got along fine after a few adjustments. Then he put in a Baptist, Presbyterian, and Catholic; soon, there was not a living thing left. I think Twain in his jest was right. When it comes to relationships, we are not always good stewards. Knowing that is half the battle.

Forgiving and Restoring Broken Relationships

We can't do stewardship of relationships justice without diving into forgiveness and restoration a little deeper. We have a responsibility to do our part in all the relationships God brings into our lives and forgiveness is core as believers.

As believers, we don't have the luxury of doing what the world does, simply writing people off at the first sign of offense or trouble. If you do, much like other areas of your stewardship life with God, you are just fooling yourself. You are no different than the world and just playing church if you aren't engaged in pursuing and bridging gaps with people. If you can't say you're sorry until the other person does, you are dead in the water spiritually and have a lot more "waxing the car" to do until you get it right.

When Jesus taught us to pray, as recorded in Luke, He says,

"Forgive us our sins as we forgive those who sin against us." In Matthew 6:14-15, at the end of the Lord's prayer, He says, "For if you forgive others their trespasses, your heavenly Father will also forgive you, but if you do not forgive others their trespasses, neither will your Father forgive your trespasses." In short, if we don't let it go, we are condemning ourselves.

In my first book, *Deep Water*, I spent time reflecting on and sharing on the topic of forgiveness. What occurred to me when writing this book, and this section surrounding forgiveness in particular, is that it really does take letting go. Ironically, forgiveness of an offense doesn't set the offender free, but the person doing the forgiving is set free. It is like a vaccine for the heart for the forgiver. Or better, a cure. Not only is there a release of the soul, but it immunizes you from future assaults and injuries. Forgiveness gets easier. Conversely, unforgiveness is like a cancer that grows and metastasizes and will eventually infect all the relationships around you. Human history confirms this. Brother against brother, and nation against nation. Intergenerational conflict can go on for years or centuries all because of unforgiveness. How ironic that Christianity's one unique differentiator from all other religions is grace.

Forgiveness is contrary to our nature. In an age when we all want justice for ourselves but hold it back for others, it is next to impossible to arrive at a place where we could surrender our broken hearts, feelings, and much worse, to simply let go. Pride gets in the way, and relationships are permanently destroyed. The negative impact can be far-reaching.

What do I mean by letting go? Not that you forget the offense, but that you simply look past it, put *self* aside, and show mercy. Letting go is arriving at a place where we no longer need justice as we perceive it but realize we have a part to play in resolving conflict. We don't forget, we simply choose to care more about something else. That something else is God's forgiveness for us and the reconciliation that we can't withhold ours. What right do we have? It comes back to God's sovereignty again. I personally arrived at a place where I accepted that no evil or injustice is beyond Him. The offense given or hurt caused really is observed and felt by God. Jesus took this on Himself at the cross and forgave it already. So what right do I have to hold on to it? I don't. It also became clear to me that He is the Ultimate Judge and not me. So I had to surrender to His sovereignty and accept that it is His and only His place to judge when He sees fit, be it now or when Jesus returns. As followers of Jesus, we are called to let it go and pursue peace with those who have offended us or injured us. In the meantime, when my flesh is warring inside me on this, I will often prayerfully say, "Lord I will sue that person in the courts of heaven some day." And then, I fight to put it out of my mind and not rehearse it over and over. If you are letting it go, let it go.

So what are we to do as a part of the act of forgiveness and the art of letting go? Well, I think it can take on three possible forms. One is doing nothing, which is still doing damage. Two is engaging in ongoing negative behavior that continues to cause harm. Three is trying to mend fences and restore, or at the very least, leave the door open for that possibility in the future. The latter for Christians should be a muscle we exercise daily and our ultimate goal should be for this to be a default in the face of offense.

Letting go means saying no to self and yes to selflessness and grace. Sure, that person offended you, hurt you, stole from you, or said things that simply weren't true. Perhaps the offense is much much worse. Rape, murder or worse. You may not even know who they are. Paul says in Romans 13:8 that as believers, we are to owe no man anything but love. We don't have it in us to do that. Not without the Holy Spirit and a deep understanding of grace.

What is the alternative? It is to go through life carrying a potato sack on your back. (I don't mean that literally, of course.) I remember years ago saying to someone in the heat of conflict that "dismissing other's feelings with their callous contempt for anyone else and selfishly pursuing what they wanted would lead to regret and unforgiveness. That regret would be like putting a twenty-pound potato sack on your back and fooling yourself into thinking you only have to carry it a little way when, in reality, you are consigning yourself to carrying that sack the rest of your life." Guilt is a heavy burden. It grows in weight over time as the shoulder tires from carrying it.

When you hold a grudge and refuse to forgive someone, you are signing up for one potato at a time to a heavier and heavier load as you march through life. My advice: Put down the sack! If God's mercy is good enough for you, it's good enough for everyone that has ever hurt you. You have no right before God to withhold mercy and forgiveness. I know that stings. But it is required of us.

Influence and Status

Every one of us has influence. God gives some more than others. It's what we do with what we have that matters. We can use it to harm others, elevate ourselves, or glorify God. It doesn't matter if you are a movie star, the CEO of a major company, a famous athlete or politician, or live in a small town and work a nine-to-five job. If you are a believer, God expects you to use your influence for His glory, pointing people to Him. The moment a lust for power overtakes you it is a slippery slope.

When speaking at the New Brunswick Teen Challenge center, something I often do, I tell the guys, "You're touching a lot of lives. As an addict, every life you touched brought pain, including your own. Now that you're a new creation in Christ, free of your addiction, you can build positive relationships as a good steward. You can influence people positively and powerfully, including past relationships. When they see the transformation in your life, God can and will restore broken relationships."

Like those Teen Challenge members, I have had broken relationships; I've made mistakes. It amazes me that God has and can rebuild those bridges and restore relationships time and time again despite my shortcomings.

The whole point of the Gospel is to redeem mankind and restore the relationship between God and man. Stewarding relationships, therefore, has to include a redemptive element. Certainly, it requires an investment of time, swallowing our pride, and saying that while I may be right, I can't restore the relationship if I don't make an effort.

Often, the truth is that while we want redemption, we don't like giving it. We want justice but don't want to extend it to others. We want grace but don't want to show it. Yet, that's exactly what we got when we became believers. If we can't model that to others, we have to ask ourselves if we truly understand the price of our salvation. God invested in restoring a relationship with us by going to extremes — the death of His Son. And Christ left the ninety-nine to chase after the one who broke fellowship —

that's our responsibility as well.

Two examples where people have used their influence to restore relationships, risking everything in the process, are Joseph and Queen Esther.

When we explored the chapter on talents, I stopped Joseph's story short of Genesis 42. I did this because Joseph was not done teaching us about stewardship.

My favorite part of Joseph's story is the restoration of his relationship with his brothers. He says, in Genesis 45:5, "And now do not be distressed or angry with yourselves because you sold me here, for God sent me before you to preserve life."

Joseph saw how God used his circumstances for good, that his brothers' jealousy and betrayal were necessary to bring about God's will. If he had not been sold into slavery or had failed to continue trusting God through those dark years as a slave, he wouldn't be standing before his family with the opportunity to save Israel from famine.

Can you imagine the tragedy that would have occurred if Joseph had hardened his heart toward his brothers? His response is grace, mercy, and forgiveness on full display. It evidenced Joseph's understanding of God's nature.

Queen Esther's story is amazing to me as well. Esther was a Jewish woman whose story is one of great courage. She rose to be the queen to the most powerful man in the world of that time, King Ahasuerus of the Persians and Medes. She came to her place at the king's side because her hard headed predecessor, Queen Vashti, bucked the king's authority. (Esther 1:12)

The king doesn't know Esther is Jewish, but he loves her and admires her beauty. Insert Haman, the king's right-hand man, a prideful guy who developed a hatred for the Jews because Esther's uncle, Mordecai, wouldn't bow down to him.

A year goes by, and Haman has had enough. He offers the king ten thousand talents — thirty thousand dollars today — of his own money to pass a law that all the Jews in the kingdom be destroyed. (Esther 3:9)

So, there is Esther. In His divine plan, God has elevated her to a queen, and now there is a plot to kill her and all her people. It seems the solution is for Esther to go to the king and say stop. But it isn't that easy. The king had to summon someone before they were allowed to appear before him, including the queen. If they went before the king without being called, they were put to death. (Esther 4:11)

Esther has God-given influence, but she was faced with the idea that using it could mean more than just loss of prestige and influence in the king's court. Esther wasn't just risking her influence but also her life to go to the king and beg for the lives of her people. She would also have to reveal that she was a Jew.

It is important to note what her uncle Mordecai says in chapter four, verses thirteen and fourteen: "Do not think to yourself that in the king's palace you will escape any more than all the other Jews. For if you keep silent at this time, relief and deliverance will rise for the Jews from another place, but you and your father's house will perish. And who knows if you have not come to the kingdom for such a time as this?"

"For such a time as this." I love those words. Like Esther, we all have a purpose in God's kingdom and where you are right now is where He wants you. He is grooming you and using your worst hurts and past sins for such a time as this.

Esther risked it all, and, thankfully, the king spared her when she went before him unannounced. Because of Esther's influence, the king saves the Jews, and Haman gets the hangman's noose that he thought he had built for Mordecai.

Esther could have tried to hide behind her status and position and not take that risk. To what end, I ask you? How many of us who God has entrusted with a place in society for a purpose aren't showing the same leadership and courage as Queen Esther? How many of us are too busy living in the spotlight, forgetting who put us there?

Conflict - Focus - Slavery

My observation is, if the church took relational stewardship more seriously, there would be healthier conflict among believers. Churches wouldn't split every time there is a disagreement. They would talk through things and move on constructively. Don't get me wrong, I know that many reading this have also had good experiences in the church with conflict. I'm focused on the vast majority of the ongoing division in the greater church that is on display for the world to judge. Which they do. It seems pride is always in the center of it, isn't it? I think we have all seen that leaders in the church often shy away from getting to the heart of issues, seeking to restore and resolve issues. They fail to see healthy conflict as constructive and instead avoid the conflict. The church is often afraid of conflict, while in the business world, we understand that healthy conflict can be a good thing. If you're moving forward, trying to accomplish something, you're going to have conflict. And the moment you put two people together, you will have a difference of opinion. Matthew 18:15-19, the passage about church discipline, would undoubtedly be practiced more if people saw conflict in a more constructive light.

More often than not, we simply sweep things, and often people, under the rug. People leave as a result, and no one matures spiritually on either side of the issue, including church leaders. Restoration and forgiveness are not achieved.

I've observed that most people don't see anything that separates the church from the world and as such aren't drawn to the church. This is not the rule, but is often the case. The church's goal should not be to be the last best hope of the world. It should be the first place people turn. Much of the time, if a church is weak at conflict resolution, and people do cause or engage in conflict, the church in its fear and reservation around conflict miss-applies scripture and shuns the people as a "carte blanche" way of dealing with it.

There are many passages on dealing with tension in the church. Titus 3:9-11, James 4, 2 Timothy 2 and many more point us to try and work out the difference and failing that, if someone isn't prepared to, then we are still called to abstain from the conflict with love. Often the problem is if people engage in conflict, it's because they want to be right rather than try to understand or find a way forward post-conflict. They may simply not be mature in their faith or as a person and need more time to get there. I've learned the best way to deal with conflict is curiosity, seeking to get to the root cause. Often the cause of the conflict isn't what it appears to be on the surface. Like Jesus, we need to ask questions. We also need to be content not to get our way or win the conflict. Pride is such a driver in the human heart and is often what causes conflict and prevents reconciliation. The mature believer may need to be the bigger person and lovingly agree to disagree and still try to move forward as best as possible, not discouraging the other party, letting the Holy

Spirit wrestle with them. So many in the church today have an internal dialogue that goes something like this, "I rejected the church for a time because I found so little grace there. I returned because I found grace nowhere else." I personally want to see our churches shine on a hilltop where imperfect people are working through stuff and the world is drawn to that unique worldview that is wrapped in God's amazing grace. Now if you are a part of a church like that, you know what to do. Send out your people to spread that love to new fronts on the spiritual battlefield. Don't stay idle. We need you. The world needs mature churches to send out disciples into the world and the greater church.

Benjamin Franklin said, "There is perhaps no one of our natural passions so hard to subdue as pride. Beat it down, stifle it, mortify it as much as one pleases, it is still alive. Even if I could conceive that I had completely overcome it, I should probably be proud of my humility."

If Christians asked a few crucial questions, so much more could be accomplished for the kingdom. Am I okay not winning or getting my say? Can I concede that moving forward is more important than being right? Am I fighting for what I want or what God wants? Have I wrestled with this privately with the Lord? Do I want restoration or restitution? Do I love the other person, or am I more interested in settling the score?

The fruit of the Spirit versus the harvest of the flesh is at play here. But from my observation, the church is often busy *doing ministry* while neglecting to actually minister to people in their midst when the going gets tough and where it really counts for something in God's eyes. It only stands to reason that the spiritual health of the people in our own churches should be important before we head out the doorstep to take on the world. Much like our families above, we need to fight for our spiritual families.

At the risk of going too far I think from a stewardship perspective, many North American churches are like spiritual "spas," accomplishing nothing of significance for the kingdom. On the contrary, these churches are doing damage more often than not, as people come out of the world seeking truth and love and get the same thing inside the church but with a shine to it. Many of our churches in the west are in this sorry state of self-deception today, and we need to get this right, or we will have much to account for when we stand before Jesus someday.

One of my biggest fears is that God will say to me, "Jonathan, my son, I had so much more for you to do, and you squandered your time with foolish pursuits." I feel like I have already wasted half my adult life building my castle while His kingdom sits in ruins, and I don't want to waste the last half. I know I'm not alone.

John Newton, the famous writer of the hymn, *Amazing Grace*, once said something very similar.

In the late 1700's, Newton was a slave ship captain who didn't become a follower of Jesus until much later in life. He came to understand God's grace and was a zealot for Jesus the rest of his days, influencing the relationships around Him. One of those relationships was William Wilberforce (referenced earlier), a young man whom Newton mentored and introduced to Christ. Wilberforce, at 23 years old, was one of the youngest men in Parliament and a good friend of England's youngest prime minister, William Pitt, 24. To this day Pitt is still England's youngest ever Prime Minister.

The seed Newton sowed in Wilberforce's life took root ten years later when the Holy Spirit led him to spearhead an abolitionist movement to end slavery in the British Empire. Slavery had always existed until one hundred fifty years ago. What God put in the hearts of His people at the time was unheard of, unthinkable to the global economy. If God's people had been divided, it's possible His will wouldn't have been accomplished at that time. There was strong opposition in and out of the church, but the key players stayed steadfast in pursuing their calling and worked through conflict within their ranks. Today, he is remembered as the leader of the abolition campaign in British history. After decades of pursuing God's justice, William only learned of the movement's success on his deathbed.

If you study the history of these events, you will find many obstacles, people, pride, ambition, and greed that stood in the way. Wilberforce encountered great resistance in and from the church. Notwithstanding that, God's people got it done because they put God's mission first, not their egos.

I often wonder, would God have brought an end to slavery without Wilberforce and the others involved in the abolition movement? It was his time. How unfortunate it would have been for him not to have a part in this historic event and for God to choose another. His best friend Pitt even said to Wilberforce, "If you don't step up, another will."

Relationship Concentric Circles

Often, people are drawn to me because, as my wife says, I am a "fountain of energy." I realize that although I sincerely want to encourage all the lives I come in contact with, I will surely burn out if I try to be all things to all people.

To help me gain perspective regarding relationships, a pastor friend taught me about relationship concentric circles. There are three: inner, middle, and outer. This was a game changer for me and I want to share it with you.

The **inner circle** consists of people with whom you are intimate, those you do life with and grow with. You trust them to speak the truth in love, encourage you, and even confess your sin to. These are people with whom you have a custodial responsibility before God. It is a small circle consisting of just a few. For Jesus, it was the disciples, His mother, and a few other followers, such as Mary Magdalene. For us, it's family, close friends, and confidants and some people in our local church or our Christian circles.

The **middle circle** is those people who are rooting for you and you for them, but with whom you may not have the same level of intimacy. You have an accountability to God for them, however, because they are in your life regularly, just not to the same degree as the inner circle. It could be a pastor with his congregation or me as a businessperson with my clients and employees. While we may not be intimate, we can still have influence.

That leaves the **outer circle**, people you may never know, but to whom your influence extends. That could include people in your church or community. In my case, it could be family members of employees or people who read my book or hear me speak. Often this includes people you will never personally meet. But you still influence them indirectly.

Each circle comes with a certain level of trust and responsibility — the inner circle requires more and the others less as there is not as much of a relational transaction taking place. The level of commitment also intensifies as you move inward, from one sphere to the other.

Here is an example that hits close to home for me. Someone that ended up being a part of my middle circle and a daily part of my life for months this past fall and winter. John is an elderly, retired gentleman I've known for a long time.

John has helped around our property for years, plowing snow, chain-sawing, and doing other chores when I don't have time. He is a hoot and always smiling. He is a guy who at 2 am would roll in plowing our property in a snowstorm smiling like a hero! I would get up out of bed and take him out a hot coffee and a banana. We would shoot the breeze as the storm raged outside the truck. I looked forward to snowstorms for this reason only! Sadly, he was diagnosed with ALS — Lou Gehrig's Disease — a few years ago, and I've watched as his health has steadily deteriorated. He lost his driver's license due to the disease. And even though his muscles were breaking down, he still wanted to do some yard work, so I would pick him up, bring him over, we would work together, and I would take him home.

Recently, John got to the place where he couldn't talk, and the only way he could communicate was through an iPad. Now, he's in the hospital in the last stages of the disease. We both love books, so I go to the hospital a few evenings a week to sit and read to him. Even though it's tiring after a long day at work, I know I'm responsible to Christ to cherish that relationship. God has put John in my path. It's not a cursory relationship either, but one where I get to influence him for eternity's sake.

I don't know how the Lord orchestrates relationships. I do know that when He brings someone into our circle, we need to view our responsibility toward them as if we're serving Christ. We don't get to pick our circles or the time in history we live, and we don't have a right to push back and say, I don't want that person, I want this person if we want to serve the times and serve our savior.

We also don't get to squander relationships and see them come and go, not realizing that God is putting someone in front of us for a specific purpose. There may be no one else there. "The harvest is plentiful, but the workers are few," as Jesus said. It's our responsibility to shoulder. People will come and go, but our job remains the same — to be a positive influence in their lives, loving them the way Jesus would.

It was Joseph's God-given influence that lifted him from a prison cell to second in command of all of Egypt to save God's people. Esther's influence over one man saved that same nation from destruction. Finally, John Newton's influence over one young twenty-three-year-old British parliamentarian saved millions of lives for eternity and changed the course of modern human history.

Never doubt the difference your influence can make for God's kingdom.

Stewarding Relationships Requires Being Deliberate

I have learned that you have to be deliberate to steward relationships in a way that honors God. Reach out to the person, pray for them, text them, and see how they're doing. Ask permission to build a relationship with them. Be proactive, show up, and speak truth into their lives with grace and love.

Don't beat yourself up if you haven't mastered this. Just keep making it a priority. Much like tithing is the training wheels of giving, loving people requires work and effort to improve upon.

The end goal is to get to a place where you speak love into someone's life and encourage them toward eternity.

Another friend of mine, Doug, who works in the film industry in LA, was experiencing a tough time during the midst of Covid. Originally from Nova Scotia, Doug had returned with his family due to the coronavirus pandemic to keep them safe. He was struggling, down and out, dealing with Covid-19's effect on his industry. He and his wife were homeschooling their children, and he was working all hours of the day remotely. They had lost several family members in tragic circumstances, but the straw that broke the camel's back was the loss of his beloved family pet, their eighteen-year-old dog, which was like a child to them.

At that rock bottom moment when the dog died, I knew I needed to be there for Doug. For a season once a week, I would get up at six in the morning and meet him in the next community over where they lived. We would go for a walk where we spent time talking about whatever he wanted. Interestingly enough, God, eternity, and how it all fits together invariably came up as topics of conversation. Most of the time, he was the one talking as he processed his thoughts. He knew I was praying for him — he asked me to. Then, we'd finish off by sharing a coffee at a local spot and head to work.

That's what I mean by being deliberate. Showing up and investing time in Doug's life because the Lord put him in mine. That's what Christ would do, and as His disciples, it's our job to model that behavior.

However, being deliberate is not the only step. Here is a process I use that you can follow:

Acknowledgment

Stewarding relationships also requires your acknowledgment that this is a relationship God has put before you. When I meet someone new, I think this may be the only time I will ever encounter them. Maybe I will get to interact with them for a season. If they are a believer, I will get to spend eternity with them. Whatever the period, I acknowledge that God put this person in my path, and it is not random. God is ordering my steps.

Accountability

I have accountability to God to be a good steward of the time I spend with the person, just like John Newton with William Wilberforce.

Analysis

Last, I go into curiosity mode: What can I glean from my interaction with this person? How can I be vulnerable to them in a way that encourages them to open up and permit me to speak into their life? How can I bring my gifts and talents to bear on the relationship in a way that edifies and builds them up so they know they have an ally in life?

THE TAKEAWAY

God puts relationships in our path for reasons that suit His eternal purposes. How we treat those reveals our willingness to be accountable as good stewards. We are responsible as disciples to model Christ's behavior, whether that's restoring a broken relationship, managing conflict, or investing time, energy, and resources to develop intimate relationships with people in our inner circle.

We may not know the outcome in our lifetime. We may have to wait until eternity before we see the part we indeed played, but we will live a full life as we do it. He promises that.

What is one relationship that Jesus had, which you would consider an ideal model to follow? What are its characteristics?

Describe a relationship where you encountered conflict. How did you handle it? What could you have done differently or better? Were you able to restore the relationship? Why or why not?

What does it mean to be a good steward of relationships?

What is one relationship you feel led to work
on prayerfully?

YOUR INVITATION

It is no accident that you have read this book. God put it in your path to expose you to something you may have never considered, that authentic biblical stewardship in its fullest expression isn't about giving ten percent of your income at church on a Sunday morning but committing your entire life to Him, recognizing His ownership and sovereignty over everything you possess.

"Who owns it?" is the motherlode question that has run throughout this entire book like a vein of gold. If we acknowledge that God owns everything, we must also recognize that it is not *what* we do in service to Him so much as *why* we do it — to glorify Him, not ourselves. Once we accept that fact, Christian service becomes no longer *work* or a chore but a grateful response to His grace, not merely fulfilling a religious duty but starting on an exciting journey.

When Jesus left the earth to return to His Father, He sent the Holy Spirit to be both comforter and enabler, empowering us to live the Christian life. He also gave His disciples, and by extension, the church, this promise:

"Very truly I tell you, whoever believes in me will do the works I have been doing, and they will do even greater things than these because I am going to the Father." (John 14:12)

As the church, we are the hands and feet of Jesus to the world, but we can only do these "greater things" if we are sold out, obedient, and engaged in action. There is no room for benchwarmers here. God's kingdom is not a spiritual spa for those who are over-churched and encourage religious obesity. It is for thoroughbreds who want to run the good race and fulfill the Great Commission.

God has created us at this moment in history to use the building blocks listed in this book. We are called to be stewards of His grace, time, talents, money, and more to touch the lives of those He brings us into a relationship with, to be Jesus to them to declare and demonstrate the Gospel.

But these building blocks are nothing more than raw resources that we can either use for selfish gain or kingdom purposes. Only when the Holy Spirit combines them with our spiritual gifts and gives us direction in their use do they have value in bearing fruit for eternity. Without His grace and the Spirit's leadership, we are nothing more than a clanging cymbal.

You are probably familiar with the passage in Matthew 7 where Jesus said, "On that day many will say to me, 'Lord, Lord, did we not prophesy in your name, and cast out demons in your name, and do many mighty works in your name?' And then I will declare to them, 'I never knew you; depart from me, you evildoers.'" Or what about the passage in Mark 11, where Jesus cursed the fig tree for not bearing fruit. Its fruitlessness led to His judgment.

The questions before you then are, "Am I willing to steward these building blocks, these raw resources, to be Jesus to those I encounter? Am I doing my part in working with God by allowing the Holy Spirit to produce fruit for eternity in my life? Or am I only using them for selfish gain?"

God may be employing this book as a means to wrestle with you just like He did with Jacob that night at the brook Jabbok, as told in Genesis 32. Can you say with assurance that you have put your faith and trust in Christ? Have you indeed said, "Yes, He owns it all"?

Complete surrender of your will starts with repentance, confessing your sin, and asking the Lord to come into your heart, take control of your life, and accept God as your father. Once you have done that, make the Word your life fellowship with like-minded believers in a local church (however broken it and they may be), and seek out leadership where biblical truth is taught and lived.

Possibly, you have read the poem, *The Dash*. Chiseled into each gravestone is the year we were born and the year we died. In between is a dash, a symbol representing our life. My question for you is, what will you do with the dash?

Psalm 90:12 tells us to "number our days that we may get a heart of wisdom."

If you knew that today was your last day on earth, what would your testimony be? That you "numbered your days" giving generously of your resources or that you lived for yourself, building a perishable kingdom?

There's an old saying: "The trouble with time is you think you have it."

The truth is that none of us knows how much time we have. When my father died due to a SCUBA diving accident at age forty-three, he didn't know he would be standing before his Creator that day. He and I headed out to the ocean, just like any other day, unaware that would be the last time we would see one another in this life. He had to give an account of his life that very day to Jesus.

Each day, I visit my dear friend John, the man I referenced in the previous pages, in the palliative care ward of the hospital. With each visit, I watch as his time on earth slips away faster and faster.

Those visits mean a great deal to both John and me, not only because I get to share precious time with him, but also because they remind me of the urgency to fulfill the Great Commission and the critical role holistic stewardship plays in that endeavor. It also reminds me of the brevity of life. John knows he only has weeks, maybe months. Most of us don't get that luxury.

One hundred percent of people are guaranteed to die one hundred percent of the time. No one gets out of this life alive. The sole decision each of us gets to make is how we will spend the time.

So, my challenge to you is: Don't squander the time you have on selfish living. Dig in and make it a priority to know Jesus and God your Heavenly Father. Embrace the Holy Spirit and make the most of your time here by investing your resources in His kingdom and glorify God with all that He has entrusted you.

When the day of your death comes, and you stand before God, what do you want to hear Him say: "Well done, good and faithful servant" or "Depart from Me, I never knew you"?

If it's the former, consider this your invitation to move from the temporal to the eternal, from perishable to imperishable, from flesh to Spirit, duty to joy, and selfishness to selflessness. It will be the best decision you could ever make. The choice is yours, Dear Reader. Eternity hangs in the balance for you and all the lives you touch.

ABOUT THE AUTHOR

Jonathan Lewis spends his working hours in the world of personal finance. As someone who deals with affluent families for a living, early in his faith journey, Jonathan was convicted on how he managed his own money and giving. He felt personally driven to dive deeper in his own personal walk with God when it came to understanding stewardship holistically. He quickly realized stewardship is a heart issue. Today, one of the byproducts of that journey is the vulnerable and transparent self-examination where Jonathan calls himself and the North American church to repentance for the way they handle God's resources. In writing this book, Jonathan dove into the Scriptures, prayerfully spoke with mentors and friends, and took a hard, truthful, and vulnerable account of his own life and giving motivations.

Jonathan lives in Halifax, Nova Scotia, Canada with his wife Sara and two daughters. Family is Jonathan and Sara's first stewardship priority under God. They also take time as a family to run the Jonathan David Wayne Lewis foundation, which helps put philanthropic donations into the hands of faith-based charities that need it most. Jonathan and Sara put their faith into action through community volunteering and outreach worldwide as God draws them into a deeper relationship with Him through giving.